Sequence I: First approaches

Sequence II: Historical background

Sequence III: The dream today

Sequence IV: Immigrants then and now

Sequence V: Nightmare Vietnam

Sequence VI: Is the dream still alive?

An ABC of the USA (I)

Work with your partner. Try to think of terms, things, persons etc. you consider "typical" of the United States. Find at least one for each letter of the alphabet.

Arkansas, Apaches, ... ______

Baseball, ... ______

C ______

D ______

E ______

F ______

G ______

H ______

I ______

J ______

K ______

L ______

M ______

N ______

O ______

P ______

Q ______

R ______

S ______

T ______

U ______

V ______

W ______

X ______

Y ______

Z ______

An ABC of the USA (II)

Suggestions:
(The underlined words/expressions can be associated with the American dream)

American / (John) Adams / Amish / Al Capone / Airlift (Berlin)

Baseball / Budweiser / Boston Tea Party / Beverly Hills / The Bronx

Cowboy / Coca Cola / Cadillac / Crack / Clinton / Columbus / California

Donald Duck / Disney-World / Declaration of Independence

Elvis / E. T. / Enterprise (Star Trek) / Equal Rights Movement

Football / Fast Food / FBI / Fourth of July / Fifth Avenue / Farms

Gospel / Gangster / G. I. / (Bill) Gates / Georgia / Gangs & Guns

Harvard University / Hamburger / Hollywood / Highway / Homesteads / Hemingway

Independence Day / Indians / Iowa / Immigrants / Inaugural Address / Individualism

Jeans / J. R. *(Dallas)* / Jefferson / (Magic) Johnson / Jukebox

Kennedy / Ku Klux Klan / (Martin Luther) King / J. Kerouac

Liberty / Lincoln / Levi's / Las Vegas / (John) Locke / Leatherstocking

Mc Donald's / Microsoft / Mayflower / Marlboro / Manifest Destiny

New York / NATO / NASA / Nike / New Mexico / NBA / Nirvana

Okay / Oscar / Ohio / Oakies / Opportunity / Outlaw / Orlando (Disney World)

Pepsi / Pearl Harbor / Pilgrims / Popcorn / Prairie / President / Prejudice

Quaker / Quarterback / Quilt / Queens / Quiz

Rambo / Rock'n' Roll / Rap Music / Racism / (From) Rags to Riches

Superman / Statue of Liberty / Stars & Stripes / Sheriff / Slavery / The Sixties

Texas / Top Forty / Tele-Evangelism / (Mark) Twain

Universal Studios / Uncle Tom / Uncle Sam / UFO / United Airlines

Vietnam / Virginia / (Silicon) Valley / VCR / Varsity / VIP

Western / Washington / White House / Wyoming / Whiskey / (John) Wayne / Walt Whitman

X-Ray / Xerox / XXL / Malcom X / Xmas / Xenophobia

Yale / Yankees / YMCA / Yuk vs. Yummy

Zip Code / Zoom

ForTune

EquAlity

Happiness

Melting Pot

LibErty

PionEers

DemocRacy

Ellis Island

New Canaan

InDependence

LAnd

PRogress

INdividualism

FrontiEr

MAnifest Destiny

ProMise

Individualism

– central concept in the way Americans see themselves and are viewed by others. The idea of self-reliance and responsibility for one's own fate has shaped American culture since the 17th century. Individualism in the US is rooted in the ideas of the Enlightenment, →Puritanism and the →frontier experience: If a person is given the freedom and opportunity to develop he/she will necessarily prosper.
The American tradition of scepticism about any kind of government (or church) restriction or interference – particularly in financial areas – guarantees a great degree of personal freedom, but it also furthers ruthless free enterprise and it renders almost impossible any attempt to set up welfare programs or legislature: "If you work hard, you prosper – if you fail, it is your own fault."
This struggle for freedom, and the tension between the individual and the community are key factors in American culture (cf. the Western) and the pursuit of the American dream.

Uncle Sam

– a very popular nickname for the American government (as well as for the American people). When first employed during the war against England in 1812, it was used in a derogative way by the opponents of the war. The term lost its negative connotations and became immensely popular when the government depicted Uncle Sam as a bearded man dressed in stars and stripes in order to recruit volunteers during World Wars I and II. Since then, this figure, as well as the term has been widely used.

Ellis Island

Located at Upper New York Bay close to Manhattan, Ellis Island was the headquarters of the US immigration authority from 1892 to 1954. It got its name from the New York trader James Ellis who sold the island to the State of New York in 1808. By 1892, the increasing flood of immigrants made it necessary for the immigration department to move from Lower Manhattan to Ellis Island. In 1898 and 1905, two artificial islands were added to the original one. Almost 20 million people entered the US through Ellis Island before the immigration authority moved back to Manhattan in 1954. In 1990, Ellis Island was reopened and is now a museum featuring documents and artifacts from four centuries of immigration.

The Puritans

– a social and religious movement within 16th and 17th century English Protestantism. The Puritans wanted to cleanse the Church of England from the remaining influence of Roman-Catholic Papism. In accordance with their wish to read the Bible literally and thus "purify" its message, they demanded the abolition of "human inventions," such as traditional mass, ornaments, decorations, ceremonies as well as the abolition of the traditional church hierarchy.
In the 17th century, the Puritans split up into the Presbyterians and the Congregationalists. Between 1620 and 1640, approximately 20,000 of the latter, more radical, group emigrated to New England and founded Plymouth Colony (1620), Massachusetts Bay (1630), and other settlements in Connecticut and New Haven. The Puritans believed that America was the promised land, their New Canaan. Later on, other groups, such as the Quakers, Baptists and Methodists settled in America.
The Puritans shaped many aspects of the American civil religion: virtue, integrity, education, work, individual freedom and communitarianism still play an important role in everyday life.
Stemming from their strict moral principles, their devout piousness, and the rejection of any kind of amusement or entertainment (open sexuality, alcohol, dancing etc.), the term "puritan" is also used to describe people with an extremely narrow-minded and conservative outlook.

Manifest Destiny

John L. O'Sullivan (1813–1859), the editor of the influential *United States Magazine* and *Democratic Review*, was a fervent supporter of the Democratic Party. In his editorials he popularized the belief that it was America's mission to democratize the world. In 1839 he declared the United States the "nation of the future," whose fate was "to manifest to mankind the excellence of divine principles, to establish on earth the noblest temple to the worship of the Most High – The Sacred and the True."
America used this belief in its manifest destiny to justify its territorial expansion (into Texas, California, New Mexico, Utah, Nevada, Arizona) as well as imperialism (in Latin America). The role of the United States as global mediator in political conflicts also grew out of this idea.

Independence Day (Fourth of July)

The Declaration of Independence was passed by Congress and was adopted by all thirteen colonies on July 4, 1776. The day was commemorated as early as 1777, and quickly ceremonies came to include parades, public readings of the Declaration, and speeches.
During the 19th century, the celebration turned into a popular spectacle with fireworks and parades in towns and cities across the US.
Today July 4th remains an important holiday – although the true meaning of this holiday is often lost in the hype. Still, the Fourth of July is of symbolic significance for Americans and is often made use of in (pop) culture. Examples include: *Independence Day* (movie and song title) and *Born on the Fourth of July* (Ron Kovic' autobiography about the Vietnam war).

New Canaan

The name Canaan in the Old Testament referred to the land west of the river Jordan that later became Palestine. It was the country to which Moses led his people when God told him to free them from Egyptian slavery. Before Moses died, God allowed him to glimpse the promised land (Canaan), which his people would ultimatively reach after 40 years of being on the move.
It is this biblical account to which 17th century writers and those fleeing to America from religious persecution referred when they envisioned the American colonies as the "New Canaan" (see, for example, Thomas Morton's *The New English Canaan*, 1637). It was the hope that America would become their "Promised Land."

Frontier

– a term which originally referred to the line of settlement – of civilization – moving westward. The historian Frederick Jackson Turner argued that this notion of expansion distinguished Americans from Europeans. When the frontier reached the Pacific in 1890, he declared the (geographical) frontier closed. The concept of the frontier is closely related to the American idea of →manifest destiny and explains the Americans' need for new "frontiers" (i.e. class, science).
Today, the myth of the frontier is kept alive in American culture (literature, the western, and science fiction genre) as well as in political rhetoric (i.e. J. F. Kennedy's speech on "the new frontier" in space).

The Stars and Stripes ("Old Glory")

– the name given to the American flag. The first flag was designed in 1777 and featured thirteen red and white stripes and thirteen stars on a blue background. The stars and stripes represented the founding states. The colors had a symbolic meaning: white stood for purity, red for endurance and bravery, and blue for justice. In 1818, Congress reduced the total amount of stripes to thirteen (stripes had been added for every new state) and decided simply to add a star for every new state. The design of the flag wasn't standardized until 1920; it presently displays fifty stars (the last one for Hawaii was added in 1960).

Melting Pot

Hector St. John de Crèvecœur was the first to use this metaphor to describe the United States. In his 1782 essay "Letters from an American Farmer" Crèvecœur wrote: "Here individuals of all nations are melted into a new race of men …" African and Native Americans were, however, excluded from the beginning. Ralph Waldo Emerson appropriated the term in 1845 to protest against the militant xenophobia of that time.
In 1908 the play *The Melting Pot* by Israel Zangwill was first performed. As a result of the nationwide success of the play, the term became a common expression.

Multiculturalism

This term originally referred to Canadian and Australian minority policy in the 1970s, it did not emerge in the US until the 1980s when academics started to discuss problems in education related to the changing society.
The term became rather popular as feminists, gays and lesbians, and members of ethnic minorities challenged the traditional North American and Western Europe cultural preeminence and asked for equal rights and opportunities.
The two competing concepts in the multiculturalism debate are assimilation and pluralism – on a cultural level they are mainstream vs. minority culture and subcultures.
On the one hand the concept of multiculturalism has achieved more rights for minority groups, on the other hand it has furthered cultural fragmentation.

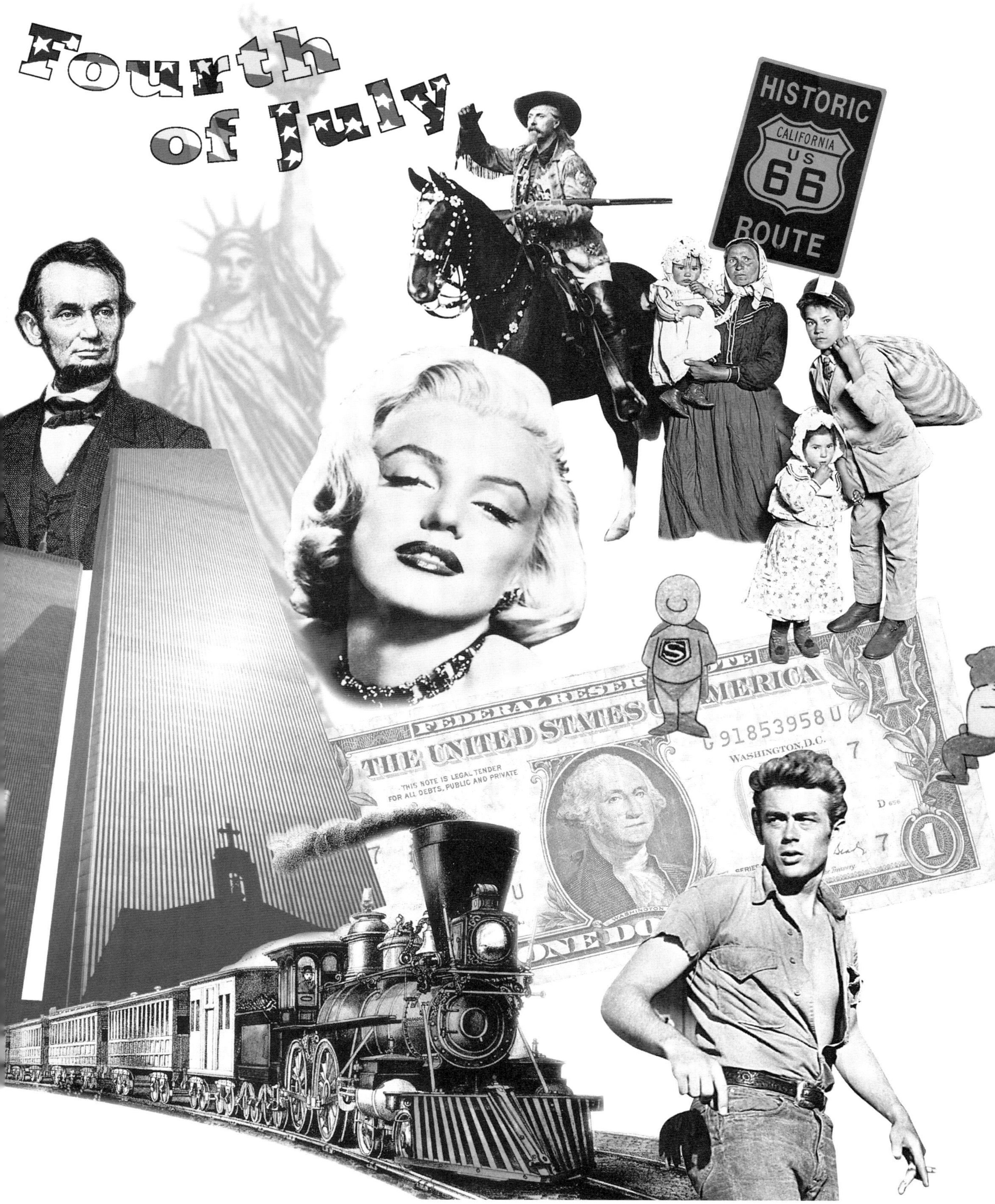
Fourth of July
HISTORIC
CALIFORNIA
US
66
ROUTE
FEDERAL RESERVE NOTE
THE UNITED STATES OF AMERICA
G 91853958 U
WASHINGTON, D.C.
THIS NOTE IS LEGAL TENDER FOR ALL DEBTS, PUBLIC AND PRIVATE
ONE DOLLAR

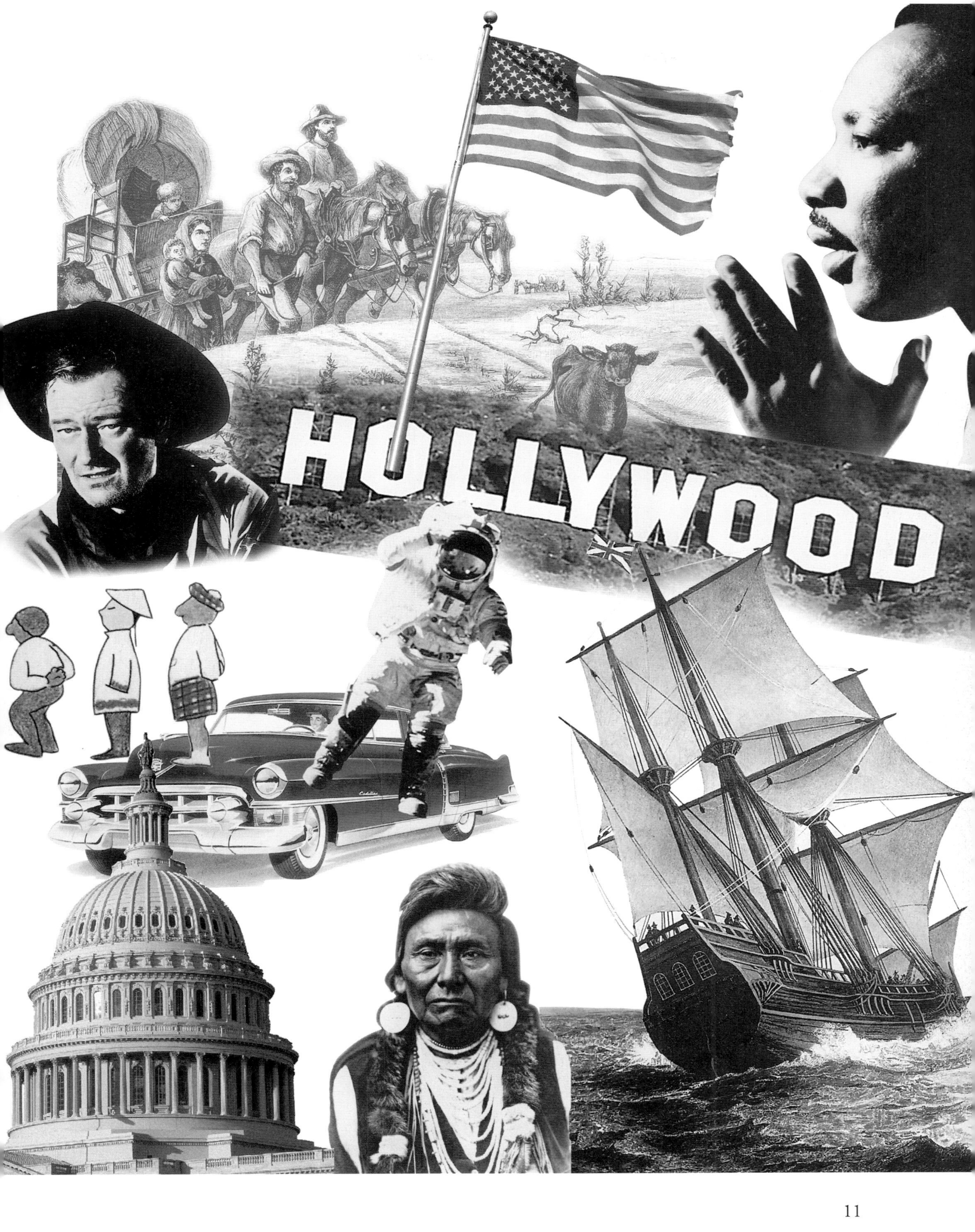
HOLLYWOOD

A 3 Images of the American dream

Tasks:

1. Try to identify each of the different elements in the collage. Work with a partner.
2. Work with your partner. Put the elements in one (or more) of the categories below.

Equality	Immigration	Liberty	Fortune

Independence	Individualism	Progress	Other

3. Explain your decision and discuss similarities and differences with the other groups.
4. The collage is called "The American dream." Work in groups of three or four. Match the elements to the different concepts of the American dream and discuss whether – in your opinion – they fit into the collage or not. Present your findings in class.
5. Which other pictures, people etc. could be added to this collection?
   Under which of the categories would you put them?

   ____

   ____

6. Now, think of persons, symbols, and things which portray negative aspects of the United States.

   ____

   ____

7. Projects (work with your neighbor or in small groups):
   a) Try to find clippings of the things listed in exercise 6 and make a collage. Find a suitable title for it.
   b) Collect clippings which symbolize aspects of German culture, history, and everyday life, put them together in a collage, and find a title.

The American Dream: Trying to Capture a Myth

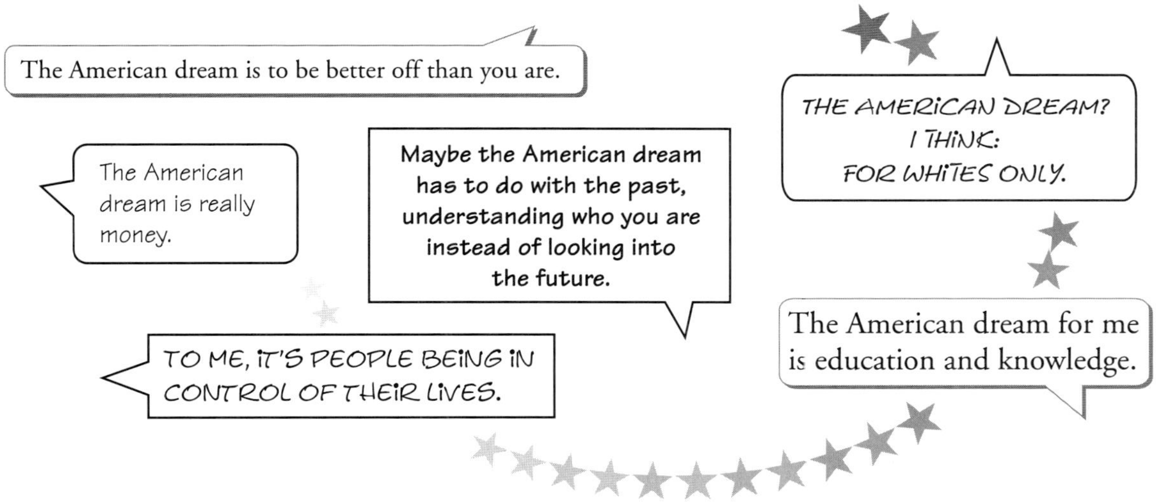

These are just a few answers you get if you ask Americans to describe or define "the American dream." But it is in this complexity and vagueness that Americans, each in their own way, can pursue their American dream. The idea, at least, is one shared by all Americans. Even if not all of them believe in it, they are able to comment on it. It is a key concept within American history, society and culture, and thus it is essential for an understanding of American society.

While no one will deny the existence of this pervasive[1] idea, one faces a far more difficult task when trying to analyze its various manifestations[2]. At the core, the American dream consists of the notion that – if a person works hard – that person will achieve his or her goals and improve his or her position in life. This is the myth that is basic to the American dream. There are many other aspects, however, that are closely related to this basic idea of the American dream. While the myth has tended to remain fairly constant, the manner of its fulfillment changes as often as American society itself changes.

In terms of religion the American dream portrayed America as a form of paradise where humankind could start anew and live in harmony with God and nature. Even before America was discovered there were myths about an "Atlantis" and a "New Canaan," that were later grafted onto the American continent.

A similar view of an earthly Utopia gave rise to ideas about how the new society and its economy should be shaped: America was seen as offering an opportunity to correct the mistakes of the "Old World:" the New World would be a more equalitarian and moral society. Here, people of different origins, races or religions would form a new classless society, which would spread democracy throughout the entire world. In the minds of Europe's poor and disowned, America was the "land of milk and honey" promising abundant natural resources, free land to till[3], and no oppressive masters or taxes. Thus, mythical America was constructed as a positive counterpart to the Old World.

The political aspect of the American dream centers around the ideas of life, liberty and the pursuit of happiness: all people have the right to pursue their goals with a minimum of state control. Government was by and for the people and should support them in their efforts to attain self-fulfillment. The belief in the rights (and the responsibilities) of the individual accounts for the United States' reluctance[4] to establish state welfare programs and to restrict free enterprise.

There are many symbols and icons which represent the American dream: The Statue of Liberty and the American flag have become the most popular ones as symbols of freedom and democracy. California, the "Sunshine State" and, particularly, Hollywood reflect the idea of material success. The West – as it is portrayed in the Western film – is a mythical place where the individual has no past and can prove or find himself/herself. The frontier, as it moved westward, came to represent mobility; an important characteristic of American society still valid today.

In order to understand the connotations in the expression "American dream" one has to consider all these aspects. And there are certainly other ideas that Americans have in mind when they refer to the American dream.

This imaginary America is, of course, not the real one. However, it is an idealized picture that sets the standard against which (not only success but also) failure is measured. When the songwriter Bruce Springsteen asks, "Is a dream a lie if it doesn't come true, or is it something worse?," he refers to the ideal. More than a few Americans feel betrayed by the promise; their lives have become "nightmares" instead of "dreams." Still, the American dream remains the standard by which to measure many of the deficits within American society.

One of the worst national nightmares was the war in Vietnam. The Americans – particularly the soldiers who fought in Vietnam – believed they fought for the freedom and democracy their country represented. However, the jungle war in Asia soon blurred[5] the lines between "good" and "bad," right and wrong. When the US government withdrew its troops in 1973, the Vietnam War had become not only a military defeat but also a traumatic experience which continues to haunt[6] the American psyche.

It is this tension between dream and nightmare, the chasm[7] between the promise and its fulfillment that distinguishes the United States from Europe, and that still determines the dynamics of American culture today.

The author

Vocabulary:

1 *pervasive* – influencing everything
2 *manifestations* – appearances
3 *to till* – to cultivate
4 *reluctance* – unwillingness
5 *to blur* – *here:* to confuse
6 *to haunt* – to plague, to torment
7 *chasm* – gap, opening

Tasks:

1. Read through the quotations and try to explain what these people could have meant.
2. Why is it so difficult to define or narrow down the concept of the American dream?
3. Name and explain one of its key elements.
4. How is the American dream connected to the idea of a "New World?"
5. Why is the dream important for understanding American history and culture?
6. Why was the Vietnam war a "nightmare" to many Americans?
7. Try to think of other symbols that represent the American dream.

1. Look at the cartoon portraying Columbus and his fellow captains having reached the American shore (still believing they were in India!)
   Work with your neighbor. What might have been the first words of this pioneer when he looked upon this new world? Use your imagination – anything goes!!!
2. Work in groups of three or four and write a short scene with the title "Columbus' first minutes in the New World."

The Promised Land

"We shall be as a City upon a Hill, the eyes of all people are upon us ...," the Puritan John Winthrop wrote. The Puritans who disembarked[1] in Massachusetts in 1620 believed they were establishing the New Israel. Indeed, the whole colonial enterprise was believed to have been guided by God. "God hath opened this passage unto us," Alexander Whitaker preached from Virginia in 1613, "and led us by the hand unto this work."

Promised Land imagery figured prominently[2] in shaping English colonial thought. The pilgrims identified themselves with the ancient Hebrews. They viewed the New World as the New Canaan. They were God's chosen people headed for the Promised Land. Other colonists believed they, too, had been divinely[3] called. The settlers in Virginia were, John Rolf said, "a peculiar people, marked and chosen by the finger of God."

This self-image of being God's chosen people called to establish the New Israel became an integral[4] theme in America's self-interpretation. During the revolutionary period, it emerged with new force. "We cannot but acknowledge that God hath graciously patronized our cause and taken us under his special care, as he did his ancient covenant people[5]," Samuel Langdon preached at Concord, New Hampshire in 1788. George Washington was the "American Joshua," and "Never was the possession of arms used with more glory, or in a better cause, since the days of Joshua, the son of Nun," Ezra Stiles urged in Connecticut in 1783. In 1776, Benjamin Franklin and Thomas Jefferson wanted Promised Land images for the new nation's Great Seal. Franklin proposed Moses dividing the Red Sea with Pharaoh's army being overwhelmed by the closing waters. Jefferson urged a representation of the Israelites being led in the wilderness by the pillar[6] of fire by night and the cloud by day. Later, in his second inaugural address (1805), Jefferson again recalled the Promised Land. "I shall need... the favor of that Being in whose hands we are, who led our fathers, as Israel of old, from their native land and planted them in a country flowing with all the necessities and comforts of life."

Joshua and the Promised Land by Roy H. May, Jr. with a Study Guide by Annette Vanzant Williams. $4.50 available in English, Spanish & Korean from the Service Center, 7820 Reading Road, Cincinnati, OH 45222-1800, 800-305-9857. See gbgm-umc.org/joshua for the entire web site.

Vocabulary:

1 *to disembark* – to leave a ship
2 *to figure prominently* – to play an important role
3 *divinely* – from God
4 *integral* – essential
5 *covenant people* – *here:* the Israelites
6 *pillar* – column

AKG Berlin

The Pilgrim Fathers signing the 'Mayflower Compact', 1620

Tasks:

1. Read through the Bible passage which describes God's decision to lead the Israelites out of Egypt. In which way did the first Puritan settlers relate their fate to the people in the Old Testament?

> Exodus 3:
> [7] Then the Lord said, "I have seen the affliction of my people who are in Egypt, and have heard their cry because
> of their taskmasters; I know their sufferings, [8] and I have come down to deliver them out of the hand of the
> Egyptians, and to bring them up out of that land to a good and broad land, a land flowing with milk and honey,
> to the place of the Canaanites (...) [10] Come, I will send you to Pharaoh that you may bring forth my people,
> the sons of Israel, out of Egypt."

2. What do you think about the concept of "God's chosen people" – especially with regard to the Americans' perception of themselves?

> Deuteronomy 7:
> [6] "For you are a people holy to the Lord your God; the Lord your God has chosen you to be a people for his
> own possession, out of all the peoples that are on the face of the earth. (...) [8] but it is because the Lord loves
> you, and is keeping the oath which he swore to your fathers, that the Lord has brought you out with a mighty
> hand, and redeemed you from the house of bondage, from the hand of Pharaoh king of Egypt.

3. Why was George Washington called "the American Joshua?" Can you see any parallels between the two men?

> Joshua 1:
> [1] After the death of Moses the servant of the Lord, the Lord said to Joshua the son of Nun, Moses' minister,
> [2] "Moses my servant is dead; now therefore arise, go over this Jordan, you and all this people, into the land which
> I am giving to them, to the people of Israel.

4. These are two stanzas of a song which is very popular in the US. Try to relate its lyrics to the concept of the "Promised Land."

Katherine Lee Bates

America the Beautiful

O beautiful for spacious skies,
For amber[1] waves of grain,
For purple mountain majesties
Above the fruited plain!
America! America!
God shed His grace on thee
And crown thy good with brotherhood
From sea to shining sea.

O beautiful for pilgrim feet,
Whose stern[2], impassioned stress
A thoroughfare[3] for freedom beat
Across the wilderness!
America! America!
God mend thine every flaw,
Confirm thy soul in self control,
Thy liberty in law!

In: Wright, Esmond. *The American Dream: From Reconstruction to Reagan.* Blackwell: Cambridge (MA) 1996, pp. 584–585.

Vocabulary:

1 *amber* bernsteinfarben – 2 *stern* streng, ernst – 3 *thoroughfare* (Durchgangs-)Straße

The Declaration of Independence

AKG Berlin

The Declaration of Independence was approved by the Continental Congress on July 4, 1776. The Congress, set up in 1774, was made up of representatives of the thirteen colonies, and its importance had increased as the relationship between Britain and the colonies deteriorated[1] to the point of war. By the time the Continental Congress formed a sub-committee to consider the issue of independence, fighting had already begun and a "Continental Army" had been formed under the command of George Washington. The sub-committee was presided over by John Hancock and included Thomas Jefferson, John Adams, Benjamin Franklin, as well as 52 other members.

Much of the text, which was drafted by Jefferson, is concerned with justifying the split from Britain, but of more lasting importance was the opening passage establishing a framework of political philosophy and principles for the new republics. The Declaration explicitly mentions the independence of the thirteen states from each other as well as from Britain. For more than ten years they were, united by mutual interest, in a confederation – a period of considerable democratic experimentation.

Vocabulary:

1 *to deteriorate* – to get worse

When in the course of human events, it becomes necessary for one people to dissolve the political bands which have connected them with another, and to assume[1] among the powers of the earth, the separate and equal station[2] to which the laws of nature and nature's God entitle them, a decent respect to the opinions of mankind requires that they should declare the causes which impel[3] them to separation.

We hold these truths to be self-evident, that all men are created equal, that they are endowed[4] by their Creator with certain unalienable[5] rights, that among these are life, liberty, and the pursuit of happiness. That to secure these rights, governments are instituted among men, deriving their just powers from the consent of the governed. That whenever any form of government becomes destructive of these ends it is the right of the people to alter or abolish it, and to institute new government...

We, therefore, the representatives of the United States of America, in General Congress, assembled, appealing to the Supreme Judge of the world for the rectitude[6] of our intentions, do, in the name by the authority of the good people of these colonies, solemnly publish and declare, that these United Colonies are, and of right ought to be free and independent states; that they are absolved from[7] all allegiance[8] to the British Crown, and that all political connection between them and the State of Great Britain, is and ought to be totally dissolved; and that as free and independent states, they have full power to levy[9] war, conclude peace, contract alliances, establish commerce, and to do all other acts and things which independent states may of right do. And for the support of this declaration, with a firm reliance on the protection of divine[10] providence[11], we mutually pledge[12] to each other our lives, our fortunes and our sacred home.

Maidment, Richard & Michael Dawson (eds.). *The United States in the Twentieth Century. Key Documents.* Hodder & Stoughton: London 1994, pp. 155–156.

Vocabulary:

1 *to assume* – *here:* to take
2 *station* – position
3 *to impel* – to drive
4 *to endow* – to provide
5 *unalienable* – cannot be taken away
6 *rectitude* – honesty
7 *to absolve from* – to declare free
8 *allegiance* – loyalty
9 *to levy* – here: to make
10 *divine* – from God
11 *providence* – foresight and care
12 *to pledge* – to promise

Tasks:

1. Read both the introductory text and the excerpt from the declaration. Note the vocabulary.
2. There are more words which you might not know.
   Write their German equivalents into this chart (if necessary, use a dictionary).

to approve	______________	to entitle	______________
to draft	______________	to derive from	______________
framework	______________	to alter	______________
in the course	______________	to abolish	______________
to dissolve	______________	reliance	______________

3. Work with your neighbor and translate. You may change the sentence structure.

> "We hold these truths to be self-evident, that all men are created equal; that they are endowed by their Creator with certain unalienable rights; that among these are life, liberty, and the pursuit of happiness. That, to secure these rights, governments are instituted among men, deriving their just powers from the consent of the governed. That whenever any form of government becomes destructive of these ends it is the right of the people to alter or to abolish it, and to institute new government."

4. Read through the Declaration of Independence again and mark the expressions which represent important aspects of the American dream. Explain your choice.
5. Look at the picture below. The slave trade was common place in the 18th century (as well as in the first half of the 19th century). How do you think the Americans reconciled the possession of slaves with the words of the Declaration?
   What does it say about the ideas of the American dream?
6. Form two groups; one collects arguments for, the other against slavery. Stage a debate in the 1860 Congress. You need one person who will preside over the meeting. Be persuasive!

AKG Berlin

Slave auction in Richmond, Virginia 1861

J. Hector St. John de Crèvecœur

Letters from an American Farmer

What attachment can a poor European emigrant have for a country where he had nothing? The knowledge of the language, the love of a few kindred as poor as himself, were the only cords[1] that tied him: his country is now that which gives him land, bread, protection, and consequence[2]: Ubi panis ibi patria* is the motto of all emigrants.

What then is the American, this new man? He is either a European, or the descendant of a European, hence that strange mixture of blood, which you will find in no other country. I could point out to you a family whose grandfather was an Englishman, whose wife was Dutch, whose son married a French woman, and whose present four sons have now four wives of different nations. He is an American, who, leaving behind him all his ancient prejudices and manners, receives new ones from the new mode of life he has embraced, the new government he obeys, and the new rank he holds. He becomes an American by being received in the broad lap[3] of our great Alma Mater**.

Here individuals of all nations are melted into a new race of men, whose labors and posterity[4] will one day cause great changes in the world. Americans are the western pilgrims, who are carrying along with them that great mass of arts, sciences, vigor[5], and industry which began long since in the east; they will finish the great circle.

The Americans were once scattered[6] all over Europe; here they are incorporated into one of the finest system of population which has ever appeared, and which will hereafter become distinct by the power of the different climates they inhabit. The American ought therefore to love this country much better than wherein either he or his forefathers were born.

Here the rewards of his industry follow with equal steps the progress of his labor; his labor is founded on the basis of nature, self-interest; can it want a stronger allurement? Wives and children, who before in vain demanded of him a morsel[7] of bread, now, fat and frolicsome, gladly help their father to clear those fields whence exuberant crops are to arise to feed and clothe them all; without any part being claimed, either by a despotic prince, a rich abbot[8], a mighty lord. Here religion demands but little of him; a small voluntary salary to the minister, and gratitude to God; can he refuse these?

The American is a new man, who acts upon new principles; he must therefore entertain new ideas, and form new opinions. From involuntary idleness[9], servile[10] dependence, penury[11], and useless labor, he has passed to toils of a very different nature, rewarded by ample subsistence – This is an American. (...)

* Where there is bread there is one's fatherland
** Dear Mother

The Norton Anthology of American Literature. Vol I. Norton & Company: New York 1994 (4th ed.), pp. 659–660.

Vocabulary:

1 *cord* – Kordel, Schnur
2 *consequence* – Bedeutung
3 *lap* – Schoß
4 *posterity* – Nachwelt
5 *vigor* – Kraft, Dynamik
6 *to scatter* – verstreuen
7 *morsel* – Brocken, Happen
8 *abbot* – Abt
9 *idleness* – Untätigkeit
10 *servile* – sklavisch, unterwürfig
11 *penury* – Armut, Not

J. Hector St. John de Crèvecœur (1735–1813)
born in Caën, Normandy – sailed to Canada in 1755 and enlisted in the Canadian militia – worked as a cartographer and surveyor – left the military in 1759 and went to New York – traveled in the colonies as a surveyor and trader with the American Indians – in 1769 married and settled on a farm like many American colonists did – returned to France at the beginning of the American revolution – in 1783, he returned to America as French consul to New York, Connecticut and New Jersey – went back to France in 1785 and after 1790, he stayed there for the rest of his life.

Letters from an American Farmer is a collection of essays Crèvecœur wrote on his farm at Pine Hill – they appeared in 1782 and were an immediate success, because they satisfied an almost insatiable demand for news about America and confirmed, for most readers, a vision of a new land, rich and promising, where hard work prevailed over class.

Tasks:

1. Read the text once. Check the glossary and look up the other words you don't know.
2. Find a suitable substitute for the underlined word; keep to the sentence structure.

   example: *His dreams were shattered.* – His dreams were destroyed.

   ll. 1–2: What attachment can a poor European emigrant have for a country …

   ____

   ll. 32–33: …, and which will hereafter become distinct by the power of the different climates …

   ____

   ll. 37–38: Here the rewards of his industry follow with equal steps the progress …

   ____

   l. 50: …; he must therefore entertain new ideas, …

   ____

   ll. 52–53: …, he has passed to toils of a different nature, …

   ____

3. Explain; you may change the sentence structure.

   example: *Unlike his sister he was rather shy* – In contrast to his sister / He was different from his sister

   ll. 3–4: …, the love of a few kindred as poor as himself, …

   ____

   ll. 39–40: …; can it want a stronger allurement?

   ____

   l. 43: … whence exuberant crops are to arise …

   ____

   l. 54: …, rewarded by ample subsistence –

   ____

4. What does Crèvecœur say about "the American?" Read through the text again and make a list. Use your own words to summarize.
5. This text was written shortly before the colonies declared their independence and founded the United States of America. Yet, some ideas of the American dream can already be found in Crèvecœur's essay. Give examples and explain.
6. What do you think about this letter? Discuss Crèvecœur's observations; do you agree with any of them?

Emma Lazarus

The New Colossus

Not like the brazen giant of Greek fame,
With conquering limbs astride from land to land;
Here at our sea-washed, sunset gates shall stand
A mighty woman with a torch, whose flame
Is the imprisoned lightning, and her name
Mother of Exiles. From her beacon-hand
Glows world-wide welcome; her mild eyes command
The air-bridged harbor that twin cities frame.
"Keep, ancient lands, your storied pomp!" cries she
With silent lips. "Give me your tired, your poor,
Your huddled masses yearning to breathe free,
The wretched refuse of your teeming shore.
Send these, the homeless, tempest-tost to me,
I lift my lamp beside the golden door!"

The Jewish poet **Emma Lazarus** wrote this poem in 1883. In 1903 it was engraved on a plate and mounted on a wall inside the pedestal of the Statue of Liberty.

AKG Berlin

"Give me your watch, your wallet, your credit cards . . . !"

Punch, Feb 2, 1980 (London)

The Statue:
started in 1875 by Frédéric Auguste Bartholdie in France – finished and shipped to the US in 1885 – located at the Upper Bay of New York harbor – dedicated in 1886 – height: 302 ft (incl. pedestal) – weight: 225 tons (only statue)

Tasks:

1. In what way does the Statue reflect the "American dream?" Is it an appropriate symbol for the United States?
2. Now look at the cartoon. Describe the picture. What would be a good title for this drawing?

Tasks:

1. Describe the picture. What do you think about it?
2. What does "U.S. Ark" refer to?
3. Can you read the writing? Do you know the words *ballot, compulsary, knouts,* and *dungeons*?
4. Where and with what intention could the picture have been published?
5. Think of a suitable title.
6. Where do you think has the picture on the right been taken?
7. Work with a partner.
   The woman's name and history are unknown.
   Give her and her children names and make up her biography:
   Where does she come from?
   Does she have a husband?
   Why has she come to America?
   What was the voyage like?
   What are her plans?
   Where does she want to go?

   Make her a real person!

Immigrants, 1905

A 10 The concept of manifest destiny

Manifest Destiny – The Intangible of American History

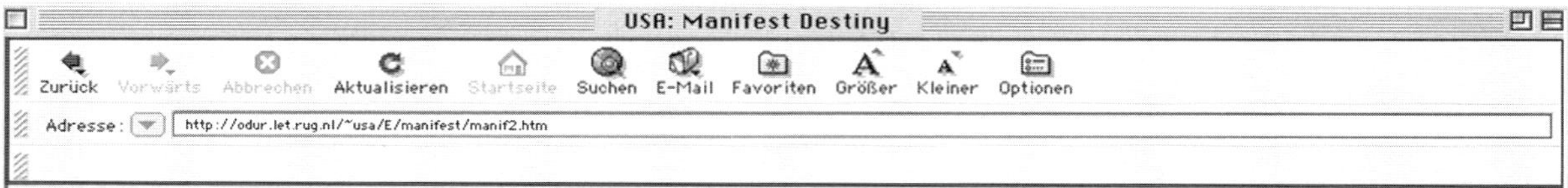

American history was built on a chronological record of significant events, each event having a cause and subsequent effect on another event. Historical events are presented in history as being tangible[1], being tied to a date, or an exact happening. Manifest Destiny on the other hand, is a phenomenon. It can not be tied to a date, event or even a specific period of time. Manifest Destiny existed and still exists as the philosophy that embraces American history as a whole. Manifest Destiny is an intangible ideology that created American history. In its simplest form, Manifest Destiny can be defined as "A Movement." More specifically, it would be the systematic body of concepts and beliefs that powered American life and American culture.

Coining the Phrase

In 1845, a democratic leader and influential editor by the name of John L. O'Sullivan gave the movement its name. In an attempt to explain America's thirst for expansion, and to present a defense for America's claim to new territories he wrote:

> *"...the right of our manifest destiny to over-spread and to possess the whole of the continent which Providence[2] has given us for the development of the great experiment of liberty and federative development of self-government entrusted[3] to us. It is right such as that of the tree to the space of air and the earth suitable for the full expansion of its principle and destiny of growth." (Brinkley 352)*

Manifest Destiny became the rallying cry[4] throughout America. The notion of Manifest Destiny was publicized in the papers and was advertised and argued by politicians throughout the nation. The idea of the Manifest Destiny Doctrine became the torch, that lit the way for American expansion. (...)

The idea of Manifest Destiny is as old as America itself. The philosophy sailed with Christopher Columbus across the Atlantic. It resided in the spirits of the Jamestown colonists and it landed at Plymouth Rock with the Pilgrims. It also traveled with the fire and brimstone[5] preachers during the Great Awakening and built the first national road. Throughout history there are numerous examples of Manifest Destiny. However, in early American history, synonyms were used to explain the not yet named phenomenon. American history books are filled with words such as, Explorers, Frontier, Territories, Expansionism, Settlers, Idealism, Sectionalism and Immigration. (...)

The Components of Manifest Destiny

The notion of Manifest Destiny had many components, each serving people in different ways. Manifest Destiny reflected both the prides that characterized American Nationalism in the mid 19th century, and the idealistic vision of social perfection through God and the church. Both fueled much of the reform energy of the time. Individually, the components created separate reasons to conquer new land. Together they exemplified America's ideological need to dominate from pole to pole. (...)

The settlements that extended across the Western territories promised the American dream: the freedom and independence of a seemingly limitless land. This, coupled with the Agrarian spirit produced an attitude that nothing was going to stand in the way of progress, the progress of Manifest Destiny. In the name of this doctrine, Americans took what ever land they wanted. With a belief that Manifest Destiny gave them a right and power to do so, many simply settled, planted and farmed Indian land. (...)

From the Beginning of Time

Manifest Destiny, in its many forms, existed throughout history. It controlled America's destiny and was responsible for man's travels throughout history. With this said, America would not be America without the phenomenon of Manifest Destiny. The philosophy that built American history was the rationalization[6] that expansionists everywhere used to justify territorial growth. Some used the Manifest Destiny Doctrine as a political philosophy stressing tradition and social stability, while others used it as a simple reason to explore new lands. Expansionists experienced minimal interference of governmental institutions in private economic activities with Manifest Destiny leading their way.

http://odur.let.rug.nl/~usa/E/manifest/manif2.htm

Vocabulary:

1 *tangible* – greifbar, handfest
2 *Providence* – (göttliche) Vorsehung
3 *to entrust* – anvertrauen
4 *rallying cry* – Schlachtruf
5 *brimstone* – Schwefel
6 *rationalization* – Begründung

Tasks:

1. How does the author distinguish manifest destiny from historical events that shaped the United States?
2. Summarize in your own words Sullivan's definition of "manifest destiny." Why is manifest destiny such an important element within American society?
3. The author lists westward expansionism as one phenomenon which was furthered by the concept of manifest destiny. Think of other examples to illustrate the consequences this idea had on American history.
4. What does the author mean with the statement "Manifest Destiny is an intangible ideology that created American history." (ll. 5–6)
5. What does the author think about the United States' idea of manifest destiny? How does his opinion become obvious?
6. Do you think the idea of manifest destiny is still present in the United States today? Why (not)?

AKG Berlin

7. Look at the picture and describe what you see.
8. Do you think this painting criticizes or romanticizes the settlers' movement westward? Explain.
9. Find a title which supports your interpretation.

The March of the Flag

It is a noble land that God has given us; a land that can feed and clothe the world; a land whose coastlines would inclose half the countries of Europe; a land set like a sentinel[1] between the two imperial[2] oceans of the globe, a greater England with a nobler destiny.

It is a mighty people that He has planted on this soil; a people sprung from the most masterful blood of history; a people perpetually revitalized by the virile, man-producing working-folk of all the earth; a people imperial by virtue of their power, by right of their institutions, by authority of their Heaven-directed purposes – the propagandists and not the misers of liberty.

It is a glorious history our God has bestowed[3] upon His chosen people; a history heroic with faith in our mission and our future; a history of statesmen who flung the boundaries of the Republic out into unexplored lands and savage wilderness; a history of soldiers who carried the flag across blazing deserts and through the ranks of hostile mountains, even to the gates of sunset; a history of a multiplying people who overran a continent in half a century; a history of prophets who saw the consequences of evils inherited from the past and of martyrs who died to save us from them; a history divinely[4] logical, in the process of whose tremendous reasoning we find ourselves today.

Therefore, in this campaign, the question is larger than a party question. It is an American question. It is a world question. Shall the American people continue their march toward the commercial supremacy of the world? Shall free institutions broaden their blessed reign as the children of liberty wax[5] in strength, until the empire of our principles is established over the hearts of all mankind? (...)

The march of the flag! In 1789 the flag of the Republic waved over 4,000,000 souls in thirteen states, and their savage territory which stretched to the Mississippi, to Canada, to the Floridas. The timid minds of that day said that no new territory was needed, and, for the hour, they were right. But Jefferson, through whose intellect the centuries marched; Jefferson, who dreamed of Cuba as an American state, Jefferson, the first imperialist of the Republic, Jefferson acquired that imperial territory which swept from the Mississippi to the mountains, from Texas to the British possessions, and the march of the flag began! (...)

There are so many real things to be done: canals to be dug, railways to be laid, forests to be felled, cities to be built, fields to be tilled, markets to be won, ships to be launched, peoples to be saved, civilization to be proclaimed[6] and the Flag of Liberty hung to the eager air over every sea. Is this an hour to waste upon triflers[7] with nature's laws? Is this a season to give our destiny over to word-mongers[8] and prosperity-wreckers? No! It is an hour to remember our duty to our homes. It is a moment to realize the opportunities fate has opened to us. And so is all hour for us to stand by the Government.

Wonderfully has God guided us. Yonder at Bunker Hill* and Yorktown** His providence was above us. At New Orleans and on ensanguined[9] seas His hand sustained us. Abraham Lincoln was His minister and His was the altar of freedom the Nation's soldiers set up on a hundred battlefields. His power directed Dewey in the East and delivered the Spanish fleet into our hands, as He delivered the elder Armada into the hands of our English sires two centuries ago *[Note – actually in 1588]*. The American people can not use a dishonest medium of exchange, it is ours to set the world its example of right and honor. We can not fly from our world duties; it is ours to execute the purpose of a fate that has driven us to be greater than our small intentions. We can not retreat from any soil where Providence[10] has unfurled our banner; it is ours to save that soil for liberty and civilization.

http://comp.uark.edu/~brmink/bever.html

* location of first major battle in the war for independence in 1775

** The Americans' 20-day-siege of the British army at Yorktown in 1781 was the last major conflict before the war ended in 1783

Vocabulary:

1 *sentinel* – guard
2 *imperial* – majestic, mighty
3 *to bestow* – to grant, to give
4 *divine* – from God
5 *to wax* – to increase
6 *to proclaim* – to announce
7 *trifler* – one who behaves lightly or not seriously
8 *word-monger* – a person who talks too much
9 *ensanguined* – blood-soaked
10 *Providence* – divine foresight

Albert Beveridge, a Republican senator from Indiana, was one of the leading spokesmen for a strongly expansionist foreign policy. He gave this speech as a campaign speech on September 16, 1898.

Tasks:

1. Read the text and write down your spontaneous reactions while you are reading. When everyone has finished working on his or her text, collect your comments in class.
   Do you agree with what others think/say about this text?
2. Look up the definition of "imperialism;" are there any similarities to "manifest destiny?"
3. This speech is more than one hundred years old; can you imagine a politician using similar arguments in the 21st century? Why (not)? Think of a situation in which such a speech could be held today.
4. Summarize Beveridge's arguments supporting the United States' supremacy of the world. What role does religion play in this context?
5. Try to summarize the most important aspects of "manifest destiny." What do you personally think of the United States' mission "[to] broaden their blessed reign (...) until the empire of [their] principles is established over the hearts of all mankind? (ll. 34–36)"

6. Discuss the United States' leading political and economic role today. Do you agree with the message of the photo?
7. Imagine Beveridge were still alive and you were his ghostwriter. What would you say about the USA today? Write a short speech (or part of a speech).

1 Bill Gates
Founder and CEO of Microsoft Corporation

born Oct. 8 1955 – 1975: drops out of Harvard University to co-found Microsoft with Paul Allen – 1980: licenses MS-DOS to IBM for its first PC – 1986: becomes a billionaire at age 31 with the company IPO – 1990: releases Windows 3.0, a hit, user-friendly answer to Mac OS – publishes a book in 1995: *The Road Ahead* → bestseller – 1995–96: markets *Windows95* and *Internet Explorer* browser – 1998: Justice Department files an antitrust suit against Microsoft – in 1999, it becomes the first company to top $500 billion in market value, equal to the ninth-largest economy in the world

dpa, Stuttgart

2 Whoopi Goldberg
Actress

dpa, Stuttgart

Caryn Johnson – born Nov. 1949 in New York – first appears onstage at 8 – high school dropout – alleged drug addiction → rehabilitation – marries – daughter Alexandra – divorce – goes to California in 1975 – works as bricklayer, bank teller, funeral parlor cosmetician – joins several theater groups – *The Spook Show* becomes a hit Broadway show → Grammy – stars in Steven Spielberg's *The Color Purple* (novel by Alice Walker) → Golden Globe – Oscar for *Ghost* (1990) – *Sister Act, Star Trek: The Next Generation, Corrina, Corrina* etc. – NAACP's 1991 Entertainer of the Year – is involved in programs for the homeless, human rights, against drugs, AIDS – hosts 1992 Grammy Awards and 1994 & 1996 Academy Awards – is one of the most highly paid actresses in Hollywood

3 Estee Lauder
Cosmetics Empress and Founder of Estee Lauder Companies Inc.

Josephine Esther Mentzer, daughter of Austro-Hungarian immigrants – born in New York City on July 1 around 1910 – father owns hardware store in Queens – Estee starts by selling skin creams mixed together by her uncle, a chemist – marries Joseph Lauter in 1930 (later changed) – opens her first office in New York in 1944 – gets counter space at Saks Fifth Avenue in 1948 – launches her first scent *Youth Dew* in 1953 – highly creative, ambitious and personal selling approach – sells her products in over 100 countries (net sales: $3.38 billion (1997) – over 15,000 employees – in 1982, son Leonard succeeds her as CEO (chief executive officer)

dpa, Stuttgart

SOCIAL MOBILITY IN THE UNITED STATES

While other societies can crackle[1] with class envy, the US often seems unnervingly free of the green-eyed monster. Bill Gates is derided as a nerd, but never begrudged his multi-million-dollar fortune. Fortune magazine's Top 400 list of wealthiest Americans is meant to be placed on the mantlepiece[2], not pinned to a dartboard. Long before *Hello!* magazine, the US television's *Lifestyles of the Rich and Famous* was gazing in awe at the ranches, private jets and stretched Mercs of the super-wealthy. The message of the programme is look and learn, not look and puke. Americans show little sympathy for schemes designed to narrow the chasm between rich and poor or to dip, however slightly, into the fortune of the very best off. Even during the Depression, Americans never made redistribution[3] of wealth a slogan. Instead they have accepted that those at the top will earn a whole lot more than they do, whether it is the chief executive of MCI pocketing an annual bonus of telephone number proportions or Michael Jordan bagging[4] a salary large enough to feed a small African republic.

One would imagine the reverse to be true: America the place where resentment would reach blood-boiling point. After all, the US is surely the land of grotesque inequality, of Beverly Hills and South Central, of Park Avenue and the Bronx. It is the place captured so memorably by Tom Wolfe in the *Bonfire of the Vanities*, where the rich and poor live in separate worlds, those with cash spending pots of it to 'insulate' themselves from those who have less. From air-conditioned home to air-conditioned car to air-conditioned office. They never even breathe the same air.

This is not a complete exaggeration. The numbers show America to be the most economically unequal country in the industrialised world. It is now common for a corporate US chief executive to be on a million-dollar salary, earning at least forty times as much as one of his ordinary employees. According to some measures, the US is simultaneously the richest country in the developed world and the one with the highest proportion of people living in poverty.

And yet Americans seem quite happy with this state of affairs. When the British Social Attitudes Survey asked workers in eight countries whether large differences in income were necessary for economic prosperity, 37 per cent of Americans said they were. Similar polls show hardly any Americans believe the government should close the gap between rich and poor. How come? The easy answer is that the US is a wealthier country than the other seven, and that to be badly off there is probably a better fate than being 'comfortable' in, let's say, southern Italy. On this logic, the 18 per cent of Americans defined as 'poor' in that they have less than half the medium income of a very rich society: in absolute terms, they are not poor at all.

But such an answer is cheating a little – and it misses the more interesting point. Americans accept great inequality not just because their overall standard of living is high, but for a much deeper reason, one that forms a key part of their national myth. It is the American dream – the belief that everyone has a fair shot at the top. Rags alongside riches are tolerable when you believe anybody can make the leap[5] from one to the other in a lifetime. Never mind your surname, your accent or your hometown. Never mind what your parents did or how much money they had. You can reach the top. The phrase may seem ludicrous – or ironic – outside the US, but the American dream still exercises a firm grip on the nation's imagination.

The watchword is mobility. Americans do not demand equality of rich and poor, just free movement between them. What they dislike are fixed, hereditary[6] classes determined from birth and closed to outsiders. If someone works hard and has talent, then no prize should be out of reach.

That at least is the ideal, written into the founding documents of the new nation. It forms the first, post-preamble sentence of the Declaration of Independence: 'We hold these truths to be self-evident, that all men are created equal.' The Founders were adamant[7] there should be no hereditary ruling class, like the one they had left behind in England. That's why they insisted the head of state be referred to as nothing grander than Mr. President.

So much for the founding ideal. But how much of the American dream of classlessness and social mobility is reality today? At first glance, it does not look good. The big families may be shamelessly new money in origin but they are hereditary dynasties all the same.

The US has an aristocracy of sorts, whether it is the Kennedys, the Pulitzers or the Vanderbilts. More mundanely, America's upper middle class locks in its good fortune, so that well-to-do families live in good areas, where good state schools train their children for entry to the best colleges from where those children can repeat, and build on, the economic success they have inherited. Meanwhile, the child born in the ghetto, raised by a lone parent on a welfare cheque, is all but sentenced from birth to a lifetime trapped in the cycle of dependency.

Little movement here from rags to riches, and not much traffic the other way either. Yet that sketch does not tell the whole story. In fact, the modern US can still boast[8] remarkable social mobility. One statistic makes the case almost alone: of all the people in the bottom fifth of the US income scale in 1975, only five per cent were still there in 1991. To put it another way, within a decade and a half 95 per cent of the American poor were poor no more. From the top branches of the money-tree comes similar proof of social mobility: four out of every five US millionaires made their pile from scratch. Recent evidence showing a slow-down in mobility from the very bottom – with the poorest finding it harder to climb out of abject[9] poverty – has done little to dim at confidence. You see it still, in the Americans flipping burgers or waiting tables, all sharing the faith that one day they will move to bigger and better things. Hollywood likes the coat-check girl who dreams of being 'in pictures'. And every day there is another rags-to-riches story to prove it can be done, from Madonna to Magic Johnson to Bill Clinton. (...)

In the US, rich and poor are separated much less by the subtle, inherited distinctions – the tribal markings – which identify rank in Europe. While class in Britain is defined by a battery of traits that have nothing to do with raw cash, America's social divide is essentially about money.

Tom Wolfe articulated the difference on a visit to Las Vegas: 'At Monte Carlo there are still Wrong Forks, Deficient Accents, Poor Tailoring, Gauche Displays, Nouveau Richness, Cultural Aridity – concepts unknown in Las Vegas.' If James Bond hoofed up on the Strip he would not order a Martini, shaken or stirred. He would ask for a Diet Sprite in a Big Gulp cup. Despite *Indecent Proposal*, Robert Redford would not pad around[10] in a tux. If he turned up dressed like that, the punters[11] would either think he was nuts or ask him to change $ 20 for the video poker machine. The dress code in Sin City is strictly egalitarian: T-shirt, baseball cap, jeans. Las Vegas is not a classy place. How could it be? Just like America, it has no class.

Bereft of the usual signs of status Americans lack the machinery of deference. Alexis De Tocqueville noticed that the masses there were free of the 'servile tradition' of the old feudal societies of Europe, touching their forelock to no one.

Of course, America's classlessness does not come without cost. The absence of both the hereditary aristocracy and the proletariat has deprived the US of the values traditionally associated with each group: paternalism and socialism. Between them, those twin forces set up the welfare state in Europe. Starting with Disraeli in Britain and Bismarck in Germany, old-fashioned paternalists laid the foundations for a system of provision and public services which social democrats, trade unionists and socialists worked to expand. Both class-dominated groups wanted benign[12] governments to take care of the badly-off through public housing, child benefit, pensions, unemployment pay, state-funded jobs and a national health service.

But in the US there was no nobility to advocate state-sponsored noblesse oblige – and no conscious working class to demand it. There was no group at the top offering to help those at the bottom because few Americans have ever accepted that society *has* a permanent top or bottom. The result is that the US lacks public provisions that Europeans regard as basic. The American ideal has centred not on protecting the poor, but on giving them the chance to become rich. (...)

JONATHAN FREEDLAND

Observer Review, July 5 1998 © The Observer

Vocabulary:

1 *to crackle – here:* to be deeply divided
2 *mantlepiece* – shelf above a fireplace
3 *redistribution* – new allocation
4 *to bag – here:* to make
5 *leap* – jump
6 *hereditary* – passed on as a right from parent to child
7 *adamant* – unyielding, determined
8 *to boast* – to speak proudly of
9 *abject* – mean, severe
10 *to pad around – here:* to walk
11 *punter* – professional gambler
11 *benign* – gracious, kind

Tasks:

1. *(= Pre-reading activity)* This is the first paragraph of the newspaper article. Fill in the missing words. You may use each word in the list just once. Work with your neighbor.

   puke – redistribution – mantlepiece – annual – lifestyles – envy – chief – nerd – chasm

   While other societies can crackle with class ______________, the US often seems unnervingly free of the green-eyed monster. Bill Gates is derided as a ______________, but never begrudged his multi-million-dollar fortune. *Fortune* magazine's Top 400 list of wealthiest Americans is meant to be placed on the ______________, not pinned to a dartboard. Long before *Hello!* magazine, the US television's ______________ *of the Rich and Famous* was gazing in awe at the ranches, private jets and stretched Mercs of the super-wealthy. The message of the programme is look and learn, not look and ______________. Americans show little sympathy for schemes designed to narrow the ______________ between rich and poor or to dip, however slightly, into the fortune of the very best off. Even during the Depression, Americans never made ______________ of wealth a slogan. Instead they have accepted that those at the top will earn a whole lot more than they do, whether it is the ______________ executive of MCI pocketing an ______________ bonus of telephone number proportions or Michael Jordan bagging a salary large enough to feed a small African republic.

2. What could this article be about? Work with your partner and find a suitable headline.

   ____

3. Now read through the entire text. Look up the unknown words and write down ten that you consider important and would like to learn. Discuss your choice in class.
4. Work with your neighbor and find suitable headings for four paragraphs of your choice.

   a) lines ______________________________

   b) lines ______________________________

   c) lines ______________________________

   d) lines ______________________________

5. Now summarize Freedland's key statements in your own words and write them down.
6. What is the Germans' attitude towards the "rich and famous?" Write a letter to the editor in which you state and explain your personal opinion on the topics discussed in the text.

A 13 An ordinary success story

(1)
Marinela's mother washed glassware in a hospital laboratory and was determined that her youngest daughter get a good education. (...) Marinela is a thin, striking, 33-year-old woman with long black hair and a nonstop smile. She arrived in the Los Angeles area in 1973 with her mother. A shy 12-year-old, who spoke only Spanish, she found herself in a suburban school where most students spoke only English.

"I was in seventh grade, and I didn't understand anything," she explains.

(2)
After graduating from Simi Valley High School, Marinela went to Cal State Northridge. "I wanted to be a chemist, like one of the people in the laboratory where my mother had worked in El Salvador." But after two years, Marinela dropped out to marry a chemist and start a family.

(3)
Once Marinela began intensive English lessons, she learned quickly. At the end of junior high, she was in honors classes and by ninth grade, she was placed in a program for outstanding students called *The Athenians.* "We went on a field trip to Cal State Northridge (part of the California state university system) and I remember the people there saying, 'After highschool you can go to college.' Americans take these things for granted, but as a foreigner and a minority, I had no idea I could do that. For me, that information about college was like a door opening."

(4)
Nevertheless, Marinela realizes that education – her own – is the only route to success in America. This fall, she returned to Cal State at Northridge to finish her studies. "It's my dream to get a degree. It's what I believe in. I put my education on hold for years so I could give my boys a good start."

Now it's Marinela's turn.

(5)
Marinela, recently divorced, has been teaching her sons Spanish at home. "I wanted them to be proficient in one language before learning another. Their father is Chinese-American so they have a mixed background. I want them to be American, feel American – not like me. I live here. I'm a citizen. I cook chicken like an American, but I was born in El Salvador. I'm always going to be different."

(6)
When she was a little girl in El Salvador during the military coups of the 1960s, Marinela Sue-Ho Reyes of Canoga Park, California, would hear gunfire at night and sometimes pass dead bodies on her way to school in the morning. "My mother and I lived in San Salvador, the capital," she recalls. "At night, I'd get under my bed because of the bombings. Life was hard and there was never enough food on the table. Americans don't appreciate what they have. We didn't even have a telephone; we only knew one or two people who did."

Tasks:

1. The text is divided into six paragraphs. Cut them out and put them into the correct order. Work with your neighbor and compare your text with the others.
2. Read through the text again. What kind of readership is it aimed at? Why?
3. Find a suitable title which fits the style of the text.

One Mom's Pursuit of the American Dream

When she was a little girl in El Salvador during the military coups of the 1960s, Marinela Sue-Ho Reyes of Canoga Park, California, would hear gunfire at night and sometimes pass dead bodies on her way to school in the morning. "My mother and I lived in San Salvador, the capital," she recalls. "At night, I'd get under my bed because of the bombings. Life was hard and there was never enough food on the table. Americans don't appreciate what they have. We didn't even have a telephone; we only knew one or two people who did."

Marinela's mother washed glassware in a hospital laboratory and was determined that her youngest daughter get a good education. (...) Marinela is a thin, striking, 33-year-old woman with long black hair and a nonstop smile. She arrived in the Los Angeles area in 1973 with her mother. A shy 12-year-old, who spoke only Spanish, she found herself in a suburban school where most students spoke only English.

"I was in seventh grade, and I didn't understand anything," she explains. (...)

Once Marinela began intensive English lessons, she learned quickly. At the end of junior high, she was in honors classes and by ninth grade, she was placed in a program for outstanding students called The Athenians. "We went on a field trip to Cal State Northridge (part of the California state university system) and I remember the people there saying, 'After highschool you can go to college.' Americans take these things for granted, but as a foreigner and a minority, I had no idea I could do that. For me, that information about college was like a door opening."

After graduating from Simi Valley High School, Marinela went to Cal State Northridge. "I wanted to be a chemist, like one of the people in the laboratory where my mother had worked in El Salvador." But after two years, Marinela dropped out to marry a chemist and start a family. (...)

Marinela, recently divorced, has been teaching her sons Spanish at home. "I wanted them to be proficient in one language before learning another. Their father is Chinese-American so they have a mixed background. I want them to be American, feel American – not like me. I live here. I'm a citizen. I cook chicken like an American, but I was born in El Salvador. I'm always going to be different."

Nevertheless, Marinela realizes that education – her own – is the only route to success in America. This fall, she returned to Cal State at Northridge to finish her studies. "It's my dream to get a degree. It's what I believe in. I put my education on hold for years so I could give my boys a good start."

Now it's Marinela's turn.

DIANNE HALES

Good Housekeeping, October 1994, pp. 218 + 220

Tasks:

1. Explain the following institutions.

   boarding school – junior college – elementary school – university – community college – high school

2. The following words might be useful in this context. Make sure you know them and look up their opposites.

staunch	__________	ambitious	__________
confident	__________	appreciative	__________
daring	__________	diligent	__________

3. What do you think of this article? Write a letter to the editor in which you summarize your opinion. You could, for example, write from the viewpoint of a recent immigrant or a native-born American.

Bruce Springsteen

The Ghost of Tom Joad

Men walkin' 'long the railroad tracks
Goin' someplace there's no goin' back
Highway patrol choppers comin' up over the ridge
I'll sleep on a campfire under the bridge

Shelter line stretchin' 'round the corner
Welcome to the new world order
Families sleeping in their cars in the Southwest
No home, no job, no peace, no rest

The highway is alive tonight
But nobody's kiddin' nobody about where it goes
I'm sittin' down here in the campfire light
Searchin' for the ghost of Tom Joad

He pulls a prayer book out of his sleeping bag
Preacher lights up a butt and takes a drag
Waitin' for when the last shall be first
And the first shall be last
In a cardboard box 'neath the underpass
Got a one-way-ticket to the promised land
You got a hole in your belly and a gun in your hand
Sleepin' on a pillow of solid rock
Bathin' in the city aqueduct

The highway is alive tonight
Where it's headed everybody knows
I'm sittin' down here in the campfire light
Waitin' on the ghost of Tom Joad

Now Tom said: "Mom, wherever there's
A cop beatin' a guy
Wherever a hungry newborn baby cries
Wherever there's a fight 'gainst blood
And hatred in the air
Look for me, Mom, I'll be there
Wherever there's somebody
Fightin' for a place to stand
Or a decent job or a helpin' hand
Wherever somebody's strugglin' to be free
Look in their eyes, Mom, you'll see me

Well, the highway is alive tonight
But nobody's kiddin' nobody about where it goes
I'm sittin' down here in the campfire light
With the ghost of old Tom Joad."

Men walkin' 'long the ________ tracks
Goin' someplace there's no goin' ________
Highway patrol choppers[1] comin' up over the ridge[2]
I'll sleep on a campfire under the ________

Shelter[3] line stretchin' 'round the ________
Welcome to the new world order
________ sleeping in their cars in the Southwest
No home, no ________, no peace, no rest[4]

The ________ is alive tonight
But nobody's kiddin'[5] nobody about where it goes
I'm sittin' down here in the ________ light
Searchin' for the ghost of Tom Joad

He pulls a prayer book out of his ________ bag
Preacher lights up a butt[6] and takes a drag[7]
Waitin' for when the last shall be ________
And the first shall be ________
In a cardboard[8] box 'neath the underpass[9]
Got a one-way-ticket to the promised ________
You got a hole in your belly[10] and a gun in your ________
Sleepin' on a pillow of solid rock
Bathin' in the ________ aqueduct

The ________ is alive tonight
Where it's headed[11] everybody knows
I'm sittin' down here in the ________ light
Waitin' on the ghost of Tom Joad

Now Tom said: "Mom, ________ there's
A cop beatin' a guy
Wherever a hungry newborn ________ cries
Wherever there's a fight 'gainst blood
And hatred in the ________
Look for me, Mom, I'll be ________
Wherever there's somebody
Fightin' for a ________ to stand
Or a decent[12] job or a helpin' hand
Wherever somebody's strugglin'[13] to be ________
Look in their eyes, Mom, you'll see me

Well, the ________ is alive tonight
But nobody's kiddin' nobody about where it goes
I'm sittin' down here in the ________ light
With the ghost of old Tom Joad."

1 *chopper* – helicopter
2 *ridge* – highest part of a mountain or hill
3 *shelter* – place for the homeless
4 *rest* – pause
5 *kidding* – giving a false impression
6 *butt* – end of a cigarette
7 *drag* – draw
8 *cardboard* – thick "paper"
9 *underpass* – under a bridge
10 *belly* – stomach
11 *headed* – going
12 *decent* – good
13 *struggling* – fighting

Tasks:

1. *(= Pre-reading activity)* Take 3–5 minutes and write down everything that comes to mind when you think of "poverty."
2. Listen to the song and write down the words/phrases you understand. Collect them on the board and summarize the bits and pieces of information about the story that are available.
3. While you are listening to the song again, try to fill in the missing words. You might want to go through the song twice. "Reconstruct" the complete lyrics in class.
4. Compare your words and phrases in exercise 1 with the text – any similarities?
5. Springsteen uses several expressions which are typical of informal language. Work with your neighbor and try to find as many as possible. Find "formal substitutes" for the words and phrases. Present your findings in class.

informal word/phrase	*in German*	*formal substitute*
______	______	______
______	______	______
______	______	______
______	______	______
______	______	______

6. Describe the characters (excluding Tom Joad) in Springsteen's song in your own words.
7. Tom Joad is the main character in John Steinbeck's novel *The Grapes of Wrath* written in 1939. It tells the story of an Oklahoman family which is forced to move to California because of the dust storms and the draught in the Midwest during the depression years. Why do you think Springsteen makes use of the novel in his song?
8. *The Grapes of Wrath* is a very popular book in the US. Its title is a reference to a quotation from the Bible (Revelation 14:19). Explain the biblical imagery and relate it to Springsteen's song.

> "Still another angel, who had the charge of fire, came from the altar and called in a loud voice to him who had the sharp sickle, 'Take your sharp sickle and gather the clusters of grapes from the earth's vine, because its grapes are ripe.' The angel swung the sickle on the earth, gathered its grapes and threw them into the great winepress of God's wrath. They were trampled in the winepress outside the city, and blood flowed out of the press, ..."
>
> *sickle* – Sichel; *grape* – (Wein-)Traube; *wrath* – Zorn

9. Try to picture Tom Joad in Springsteen's song. What kind of person is he?
10. Write a review for a music magazine about the title song of Springsteen's 1995 album. Comment on the music, the atmosphere, the lyrics, and summarize your personal opinion.
11. Work in groups: Create an imaginative poster for this song. Decide what should be in it and what the exact layout should be. Describe your poster to the other groups in such a way that they can picture it in their minds.

Michael Montfort, Hollywood

Mik Jago, Israel

Tasks:

1. Describe the pictures.
2. What do you think of them?
3. What is ironic about the photo?
4. Try to come up with a suitable caption (= title) for the photo and the cartoon.
5. What do both pictures have in common?
6. What is the photographer's/the cartoonist's intention?
7. Work with a partner. Have a close look at the two people in the photo. Make up their biographies. Where do they come from? What has led to their present situation? Write a short text.

President Clinton's Second Inaugural Address (1997)

My fellow citizens:

At this last presidential inauguration[1] of the 20th century, let us lift our eyes toward the challenges that await us in the next century. (...) We must keep our old democracy forever young. Guided by the ancient vision of a promised land, let us set our sights upon a land of new promise.

The promise of America was born in the 18th century out of the bold conviction that we are all created equal. It was extended and preserved in the 19th century, when our nation spread across the continent, saved the union, and abolished the awful scourge[2] of slavery.

Then, in turmoil and triumph, that promise exploded onto the world stage to make this the American Century.

(...) Now, for the third time, a new century is upon us, and another time to choose. (...)

Government is not the problem, and government is not the solution. We – the American people – we are the solution. Our founders understood that well and gave us a democracy strong enough to endure for centuries, flexible enough to face our common challenges and advance our common dreams in each new day.

(...) The challenge of our past remains the challenge of our future – will we be one nation, one people, with one common destiny, or not? Will we all come together, or come apart?

The divide of race has been America's constant curse. And each new wave of immigrants gives new targets to old prejudices. Prejudice and contempt, cloaked[3] in the pretense of religious or political conviction are no different. These forces have nearly destroyed our nation in the past. They plague us still. They fuel the fanaticism of terror. (...)

We cannot, we will not succumb to[4] the dark impulses that lurk[5] in the far regions of the soul everywhere. We shall overcome them. And we shall replace them with the generous spirit of a people who feel at home with one another.

Our rich texture of racial, religious and political diversity will be God-send in the 21st century. Great rewards will come to those who can live together, learn together, work together, forge[6] new ties that bind together.

(...) With a new vision of government, a new sense of responsibility, a new spirit of community, we will sustain America's journey.

The promise we sought in a new land we will find again in a land of a new promise.

In this new land, education will be every citizen's most prized possession. Our schools will have the highest standards in the world, igniting[7] the spark of possibility in the eyes of every girl and every boy.

(...) Fellow citizens, let us build that America, a nation ever moving forward toward realizing the full potential of all its citizens. Prosperity and power – yes, they are important, and we must maintain them. But let us never forget: The greatest progress we have made, and the greatest progress we have yet to make, is in the human heart. In the end, all the world's wealth and a thousand armies are no match for the strength and decency[8] of the human spirit.

Thirty-four years ago, the man whose life we celebrate today spoke to us down here, at the other end of the Mall, in words that moved the conscience of a nation. Like a prophet of old, he told us of his dream that one day America would rise up and treat all its citizens as equals before the law and in the heart. Martin Luther King's dream was the American Dream. His quest[9] is our quest: the ceaseless striving to live out our true creed[10]. Our history has been built on such dreams and labors. And by our dreams and labors we will redeem the promise of America in the 21st century.

(...) Let us meet the demands of our time with faith and courage, with patience, and a grateful and happy heart. (...) Yes, let us build our bridge. A bridge wide enough and strong enough for every American to cross to a blessed land of new promise.

May those generations whose faces we cannot yet see, whose names we may never know, say of us here that we led our beloved country into a new century with the American Dream alive for all her children; with the American Promise of a more perfect union a reality for all her people; with America's bright flame of freedom spreading throughout all the world.

Historic Documents of 1997. Congressional Quarterly Inc. Washington 1998, pp. 20 ff.

Vocabulary:

1 *inauguration* – Amtseinführung
2 *scourge* – Geißel
3 *to cloak* – verhüllen
4 *to succumb to* – sich beugen
5 *to lurk* – lauern
6 *to forge* – schmieden
7 *to ignite* – entzünden
8 *decency* – Anstand
9 *quest* – Suche
10 *creed* – Credo, Berufung

Tasks:

1. Read the text and choose 10 words you don't know and look them up in the dictionary. Select three and try to explain them to your classmates/neighbor. Then compare your choices.
2. Write down the corresponding noun or verb.

   example: *to use* → usage; *explosion* → to explode

l. 10: to extend		l. 33:	pretense
l. 12: to abolish		l. 35: to destroy	
l. 18: to choose		l. 57: to realize	
l. 20:	solution	l. 83: to know	
l. 31:	immigrant	l. 86:	union

3. Read the text again and mark the words and terms that are related to the American dream. Explain your selections.
4. What do you think of Clinton's speech? Explain your reaction.
5. Does this speech sound different from political speeches in Germany? If yes, in what way?
6. Now look at the cartoon, which was a reaction to Clinton's Inaugural. What does it imply?

POLITICALLY CORRECT **By Jim Huber**

John Wilson

Sport and Individual Freedom

The United States is popularly regarded as "the land of opportunity." Whether or not upward mobility really is easier in the US, the desire to better one's self is undoubtedly an American value, something to believe in. The "failure" in American culture is not the person who is second, but the person who settles for second best, not the person who has faults and shortcomings, but the person who blames others for his or her failure. This section will show what difference this value has made to the way Americans think about sports, and the way they play them.

Americans are fond of quoting a famous coach of the National Football League's Green Bay Packers, Vince Lombardi, who said "Winning is not the most important thing: it is the only thing." This attitude is a natural outgrowth of the value of individual achievement. Americans are impatient with contests in which the focus is not clearly on the outcome or, worse, which have no outcome at all (a tie). While some other cultures might think that, in the event of a draw, both contestants are first, Americans think both contestants are second. Being willing to settle for second best is un-American. Intolerant of drawn games, Americans have devised all kinds of modifications to make this outcome less likely: drawn games are impossible in basketball and baseball and extremely rare in football and ice hockey, both of which provide for "overtime" (...)

Above all the emphasis is on the individual's responsibility to make it on his or her own: "Every man is the architect of his own destiny" (Potter, 1954, p. 97). Mobility thus means something different for an American. (...) Americans regard high status as a prize to be won by the worthiest individual (Turner, 1960). Social life is a contest, in which the fittest will survive, where fitness is measured by such qualities as determination, pluck, aggression, daring, risk-taking and the like. (...) Individualism has another effect on the Americans' attitude toward sport.

It encourages the view that each person's opinions and interests are as good as another's, that all are equal before the law, that no institution is the preserve of an élite or exclusive group, that authority is not permanent. It is an old maxim of political science that where the state is weak, the law is sovereign.

This helps to account for Americans' highly legalistic approach to sport, an intolerance of ambiguity, and reluctance to admit that many things happen in sport which are neither clearly right nor wrong. (...)

This more democratic approach to sports – the idea that it is an open institution, not the preserve of a knowledgeable few – helped to account for the fact that commercial sports in the US have successfully marketed themselves as attractive to the ardent fan and the casual spectator alike. To make them family events, they are "packaged" with music, cheerleading, contests, banners, displays, mascots and the like. What transpires on the field is just one among a number of attractions. The desire to promote the event to an audience so wide it might extend beyond the knowledgeable fan also explains the American practice of instructing spectators about referees' calls, players, plays, time remaining etc., a difference of approach reflected both in live attendance and in television commentary, where producers are "constrained to act as if their audiences may not understand what they see" (Chandler 1998, p. 90).

In summary, Americans organize and play sports in distinctive ways, despite the many resemblances created by common origins and similar socio-economic conditions. Americans are more likely than Europeans to expect sport to contribute to the task of nation-building, to see in sports a measure of civic strength and dynamism, to see sport as legitimation of the values of individualism, a place where the virtues of hard work and resourcefulness clearly pay off and, if sports seem to impugn these values, to change the way they are played.

Mitchell, Jeremy & Richard Maidment. *The United States in the Twentieth Century: Culture*. Hodder & Stoughton: London, 1994, pp. 241 ff.

Tasks:

1. *(= Pre-reading activity)* Take 3–5 minutes and write down everything that comes to your mind when you think of the word "sport." Form groups of four and try to put your words under specific headings (i.e. *games – equipment – clothing – physical aspects – nouns – verbs* etc.)
2. Read the text. Then choose ten words you don't know and look them up in the dictionary. Try to memorize at least five words.
3. Find a suitable substitute; keep to the sentence structure.

   example: ll. 72/73: *Americans ... play sports in <u>distinctive</u> ways* –
   Americans play sports in <u>characteristic</u> ways

   l. 1: The United States is popularly <u>regarded</u> *as* – ______________________

   ll. 15/16: This attitude is a natural <u>outgrowth</u> – ______________________

   ll. 24/25: ... Americans have <u>devised</u> all kinds of modifications – ______________________

   ll. 57/58: ... the <u>ardent</u> fan and the casual spectator – ______________________

   ll. 61/62: What <u>transpires</u> on the field – ______________________

   ll. 68/69: ... where producers are <u>constrained</u> to act – ______________________

4. Work together with your partner or in small groups. What distinguishes America from other countries in its attitude towards sport? Make a list of the characteristics Wilson discusses.

Sport in the U.S.	**Sport in other countries**

5. Summarize the text and discuss Wilson's points. What about the German attitude towards sport? Is it different from the Americans'?
6. What role does sport play in your life? Do you like to do sports? Do you like watching it? Write a short essay, in which you explain your personal viewpoint.
7. Project (work with your neighbor or in small groups):
   Try to find an advertisement about sports which portrays the significance of sport in the US. Present it in class and put together a collage with the other groups.

Garry Wills

John Wayne – The American Adam

Why was Wayne the Number One Movie star, even as late as 1995*?

He embodies the American myth. The archetypal[1] American is a displaced person – arrived from a rejected past, breaking into a glorious future, on the move, fearless himself, feared by others, a killer but cleansing the world of things that "need killing," loving but not bound down by love, rootless but carrying the Center in himself, a gyroscopic[2] direction-setter, a traveling norm.

Other cultures begin with a fixed and social hearth[3], a temple, a holy city. American life begins when that enclosure is escaped. One becomes American by going out. We are people of departure, not arrival. To reach one place is simply to catch sight of a new Beyond. Our basic myth is that of the frontier. Our hero is the frontiersman. To become urban is to break the spirit of man. Freedom is out on the plains, under endless sky. A pent-in[4] American ceases to be American. (...)

Walk through any large gallery of American art, and you will be surprised at how little space is devoted to city life. Mountains, forests, rivers, glades, villages, farms – plenty of those, but few tenements or factories. (...)

To breathe free on the land, the real American must shake off the weight of institutions – not only of laws and government, but of schools and libraries. Emerson said that the wisdom of America would not be found by tending the gathered maxims of the past. (...)

John Wayne is the most obvious recent embodiment of the American Adam** – untrammeled[5], unspoiled, free to roam, breathing a larger air than the cramped men behind desks, the pygmy[6] clerks and technicians. (...)

The Western can deal with the largest themes in American history – beginning with the "original sin" of our country, the seizing of the land from its original owners. It deals with the waves of emigration west – trappers, miners, herders, ranchers, farmers. It tracks the racing, overlapping new technologies – the stagecoach, the Conestoga wagon, the telegraph, the cavalry, the railroads, barbed wire[7], successively improved firearms, new breeds of horse. It explores the relations of people with the land, of the individual with the community, the vigilante[8] law to settled courts. It is entirely a story of change, since the disappearance of the frontier is the necessary corollary[9] of pushing the frontier on. These themes may be exhausted in our culture, though the continuing popularity of Wayne seems to suggest that the need for this hero will call up again the kinds of the story where he operated best, and the problems native[10] to the form have certainly not disappeared.

*Wills refers to a representative poll among Americans by Louis Harris & Associates

**Adam is the biblical figure, the first man in a new world. Just as America was seen as New Paradise, the Americans – especially the pioneers – were portrayed as a new race, a new society.

Vocabulary:

1 *archetypal* – urtypisch
2 *gyroscopic* – eine Art Kompass
3 *hearth* – Herd, Heim
4 *pent-in* – eingeschlossen
5 *untrammeled* – unbeschränkt
6 *pygmy* – Pygmäe, Zwerg
7 *barbed wire* – Stacheldraht
8 *vigilante* – Bürgerwehr
9 *corollary* – Folge, Begleiterscheinung
10 *native* – having their origin in

John Wayne (1907–1979) – actually Marion Michael Morrison – American actor – born in Iowa – attends college in California – dropped out and takes different jobs – starts his film career in 1927 as an extra – first leading role in the western movie *The Big Trail* by Raoul Walsh (1930) – breakthrough with *Stagecoach* (1939) directed by John Ford – forty years of stardom and film production (more than 170 movies) followed; to name a few: *Tall in the Saddle* (1944), *Red River* (1946), *Fort Apache* (1948), *Sand of Iwo Jima* (1949), *Rio Grande* (1950), *The Searchers* (1956), *Rio Bravo* (1959), *The Alamo* (1960), *The Green Berets* (1968), *True Grit* (1969), *The Shootist* (1976) – he died of cancer.

Wayne continuously made the top ten in distributors' lists of stars and was named "favorite actor" by Americans as late as 1995 – his public persona influenced generations (i.e. General Douglas MacArthur, Ronald Reagan, Newt Gingrich, Ron Kovic).

Tasks:

1. *(= Pre-reading activity)* What do you know about John Wayne? Have you seen any movies he is starring in? What do you think of him?

AKG Berlin

2. Read the text and find the opposites of the following words.

   example: *start* → end

l. 4:	to arrive	______________	l. 18:	freedom	______________
l. 5:	to reject	______________	l. 20:	to cease	______________
l. 11:	fixed	______________	l. 39:	to seize	______________
l. 18:	urban	______________	l. 45:	to improve	______________

3. Read the text again. How does Wills characterize "the real American" and the West as opposed to the urban East.

American – the West – the Frontier	European – the East – the City

4. Compare your findings in class. Do you agree with Wills' characterization?
5. Do you like Western movies? Why (not)?
6. What are the typical ingredients of a Western? Imagine you are to write a Western screenplay: Write a short text in which you summarize the plot of your movie.
   Do you know any "untypical" Westerns in which the hero doesn't fit the image Wills describes?
7. Is the Western the embodiment of the American dream?
   Why, do you think, is the Western such a popular genre in Germany and other countries besides the US?

Man on the Moon

On July 20, 1969, the human race accomplished its single greatest technological achievement of all time when a man first set foot on another celestial body[1].

Six hours after landing at 4:17 p. m. Eastern Standard Time (with less than 30 seconds of fuel remaining), Neil A. Armstrong took the "Small Step" into our greater future when he stepped off the Lunar Module, named "Eagle," onto the surface of the Moon, from which he could look up and see Earth in the heavens as no one had done before him.

He was shortly joined by "Buzz" Aldrin, and the two astronauts spent 21 hours on the lunar[2] surface and returned 46 pounds of lunar rocks. Their lift-off from the surface of the moon was (partially) captured on a TV camera they left behind, and they successfully docked with Michael Collins, patiently orbiting[3] the cold but no longer lifeless moon alone in the Command Module "Columbia."

On the east coast of the United States it was 4:18 pm EDT. In Yankee Stadium in New York city 16,000 people rose to sing the National Anthem as they stopped a baseball game in progress. At Grand Central Station, the thousands of Sunday travelers cheered so loud Aldrin's last words before touchdown[4] were not heard. In Trafalgar Square, London announcers screamed "the Americans have done it'!" In Japan, television viewers were told "a new age has now begun". In Mission Control Houston, flight controllers came to their feet cheering, breaking a tradition of silence.

It had been nearly exactly 8 years, 2 months since John Fitzgerald Kennedy had walked up the center aisle of the U.S. House of Representatives and made the lunar landing a national goal. In his CBS News control booth, newsman Walter Cronkite could not speak. He turned to astronaut Walter Schirra and then said: "Man on the Moon!" It is Sunday, July 20, 1969. The mission has been accomplished ...

Nonetheless, a small gesture of pride in the nation was also made. Like all explorers of the past, the astronauts unfurled an American flag and erected it on the surface. In the vacuum of space and in no atmosphere of the Moon itself, there would be no wind to blow the flag – so it was wired outward.

For America, it was a stunning symbol – the flag flying on the Moon. Few who saw the image, however, would realize that it would fly there not just for days or weeks, but rather for thousands and thousands of years.

www.hq.nasa.gov/office/pao/History/ap11ann/

Vocabulary:

1 *celestial body* planet – 2 *lunar* moon – 3 *to orbit* circling around a celestial body – 4 *touchdown* landing

AKG Berlin

Tasks:

1. What do you know about the landing on the moon in 1969? Have you seen documentaries or movies about it?
2. Summarize the reaction of the public (lines 19–38).
3. Space was often called "the final frontier." What other frontiers do you know of?
4. Now, read one man's recollection of that day and Armstrong's 1999 comment on the significance of his successful mission to the moon.

> July 20, 1969: Just as if we were in the Eagle itself, my entire school was locked onto the television, following each and every detail described by the newsmen. Our hopes and fears were all evident as we sat wide-eyed at the images of the Moon as it zoomed closer and closer. As the puff of lunar dust clouded the camera, we thought that our hearts would jump out of our chests. Then came the first step. As Neil Armstrong stepped down onto the lunar surface and recited his now famous line: "That's one small step for a man, one giant leap for mankind," we were in a state of complete and utter amazement. To us, Mr. Armstrong and Mr. Aldrin were like all of our favorite baseball players all wrapped up into one package. They were the ultimate heroes. The accomplishments of these men, mission control, and all aerospace manufacturers who made this possible, brought out the pride in all of us. Apollo 11 was so right when many other things in the world were so wrong. It gave us much needed hope for the future.

The following is an excerpt of an interview given by the former astronauts Armstrong, Aldrin, Cernan and Cunningham at a press conference on July 16, 1999 at the Kennedy Space Center in order to celebrate the 30th anniversary of the Apollo 11 mission.

> *Question:* Mr. Armstrong, what would you say is the lasting legacy of Apollo?
>
> *Armstrong:* I think these guys might speak more eloquently about that than I. I have heard each of them do so in the past. In my own view, the important achievement of Apollo was a demonstration that humanity is not forever chained to this planet, and our visions go rather further than that, and our opportunities are unlimited.

5. In what way do these quotations reflect the American dream?
6. What does the man in the first passage mean when he says "Apollo 11 was so right when many other things in the world were so wrong?" (ll. 10/11) Do a little research on the 1960s in the US.
7. Describe the cartoon on the right and discuss the possible meanings of it.
8. Find a caption which fits your interpretation.

Gheorghe Chiriac / Rumänien

A 19 Video: The American dream

Tasks:

1. Take some time to read through the questions before watching the film. While watching the film, take notes on an extra sheet. After the video, work with your neighbor to complete your notes and transfer the information onto the worksheet.

- a) Which places are shown and mentioned in the first few minutes? ______

  b) Who is the speaker? ______

  c) What is Sue Graham's profession? ______

  d) What did she do before she started working in her present job? ______

  e) What do you learn about her background (education, family etc)? ______

  ______

  f) What is her idea of success? ______

  g) What will she do if she fails in Los Angeles? ______

- h) What is Angel Salazar's profession? ______

  i) Where is he from? ______

  k) What problems does he have in his job? ______

  l) Does he believe in the American dream? ______

  m) What is important if you want to be successful? ______

  n) Salazar gives an example for freedom: ______

- o) What does Nancy Flores do? ______

  p) What is her personal American dream? ______

  q) What do you learn about her cultural and family background? ______

  ______

  r) What are some of the typical traits of her two cultures? ______

  ______

  s) What does Nancy say about her friends and the city she lives in? ______

  ______

  t) Why isn't she scared of being poor? ______

Discussion:

2. Why did they pick these three people as representative Americans? Do you think their choice is right?
3. Write a short review of the film in which you summarize and evaluate it.

LOOKING BACKWARD

Picture Press, CORBIS, Hamburg

Tasks:

1. Look at the picture and describe what you see.
2. Interpret the scene. What does the cartoonist wish to express?
3. What could have caused him to draw such a picture? At whom could it be aimed?
4. Do you think the criticism implied is still relevant today?
5. Project (work in small groups): You work at a US public relations office and have been given the task to design a "Pro-Immigration Poster" for the US government.

Country of origin	total foreign-born*	naturalized citizens*	not US citizens*
all countries	100.0	100.0	100.0
Mexico	27.2	11.5	35.7
Cuba	3.5	5.2	2.6
Dominican Republic	2.5	2.2	2.6
El Salvador	2.4	1.2	3.0
Great Britain	2.4	2.6	2.2
Philippines	4.4	7.3	2.8
China and Hongkong	4.3	5.9	3.4
Vietnam	3.0	4.3	2.3
India	2.9	2.9	2.9
Korea	2.3	2.4	2.2
Elsewhere	45.2	54.4	40.2

* in percent

Annual Demographic Survey 1997 (US Census)

6. Look at the chart and make notes about the information given. Work in small groups.
7. Which of the figures do you consider interesting? Why?
8. Imagine these figures have just been released. Prepare a small presentation in which you introduce the new statistics to your colleagues at the Census Bureau. Work with your neighbor.

A 21 Immigration from 1820–1990

A NATION OF IMMIGRANTS

By the time American independence was declared in 1776, two-fifths of all settlers were of non-English origin. The first U.S. census, taken in 1790, revealed a population of just under four million people, with about 10,000 new settlers arriving each year. When the U.S. government began keeping records of arriving passengers in 1820, the majority of immigrants were from Northern Europe; by the end of the 19th century, they came largely from Southern and Eastern Europe. Today, the majority arrive from Latin America and Asia. Their reasons for coming, however – opportunity and freedom – remain unchanged.

1820–1840

The Industrial Revolution, which began in Great Britain in the 1700s, spreads to other parts of Europe in the early 1800s and, in combination with other factors, spurs emigration.

U.S. Immigration begins to rise in the 1830s, with about 600,000 newcomers arriving in this decade.

Textile production is among the earliest to industrialize.

1841–1860

Immigration soars, largely from German-speaking areas of Europe, Great Britain and Ireland.

The Irish potato famine (1845–1849) and improvements in ocean transportation contribute to the mass migration.

The Know-Nothings, a political party established in the 1850s, call for laws to stem immigration.

1861–1880

The 1862 Homestead Act offers public land free to any citizen or immigrant who plans to become a citizen.

Scandinavia, Austria-Hungary, Italy and Russia become important sources of immigration.

Between 1864 and 1869, thousands of Chinese are brought to the U.S. to build the Central Pacific Railroad. The U.S. and China sign the 1869 Burlingame Treaty to protect this immigration.

1881–1900

Italians, Greeks, Russians and East Europeans immigrate to the United States in large numbers.

The Chinese Exclusion Act of 1882 places a temporary ban on immigration from China, which is made permanent in 1902. This ban is lifted during World War II.

Ellis Island in New York Harbor opens in 1892 as a receiving station for newly arrived immigrants.

1901–1920

Ellis Island immigration peaks in 1907.

In a 1907 "Gentlemen's Agreement," Japan's government agrees to prevent Japanese laborers from entering the U.S.

A 1917 law bars most immigration from Asia and the Pacific, and creates literacy requirements for adult immigrants.

1921–1940

In 1921 Congress passes the first legislation restricting the number of immigrants on the basis of nationality. It limits the annual number of immigrants from a nation to not more than three percent of foreign-born persons from that nation living in the U.S. in 1910. Also, the total number of people allowed to enter the U.S. per year – from all areas outside the Western Hemisphere – is limited to 357,803.

In 1924 the Johnson-Reed Immigration Act creates nationality quotas based on 1920 U.S. census data. It reduces the total quota for immigration from outside the Western Hemisphere to 150,000.

The Great Depression of the 1930s and the beginning of World War II severely reduce immigration into the U.S.

1941–1960

The War Brides Act of 1946 enables 120,000 wives and children of American servicemen to enter the U.S. as immigrants.

Under the Displaced Persons Act of 1948 and 1950, and the Refugee Relief Act of 1953, an additional 600,000 people immigrate to the U.S. from Germany, Hungary, Latvia, Poland, the Soviet Union, Yugoslavia and Korea.

Airliners begin making daily nonstop flights across the Atlantic Ocean in the early 1950s. By the end of the decade, jet passenger planes revolutionize global travel.

The McCarran-Walter Act of 1952, better known as the Immigration and Nationality Act, retains nationality-based quotas for immigration, but sets up quotas for previously excluded Asian nations.

1961–1980

In 1965 President Lyndon B. Johnson signs into law an immigration act that modifies the McCarran-Walter Act, replacing the nationality-based system with hemispheric ceilings. Immigration from India, Korea, the Philippines and other Asian nations soars.

President Johnson designates Ellis Island a national monument.

The Refugee Act of 1980 provides for the admission of refugees "of special humanitarian concern to the U.S."

1981–1989

Immigration from Asia and Latin America increases, as does illegal immigration from a number of countries.

In 1986, the Immigration Reform and Control Act gives many illegal aliens a chance to become legal residents. Approximately 1.7 million illegal aliens seek legal status by May 1989.

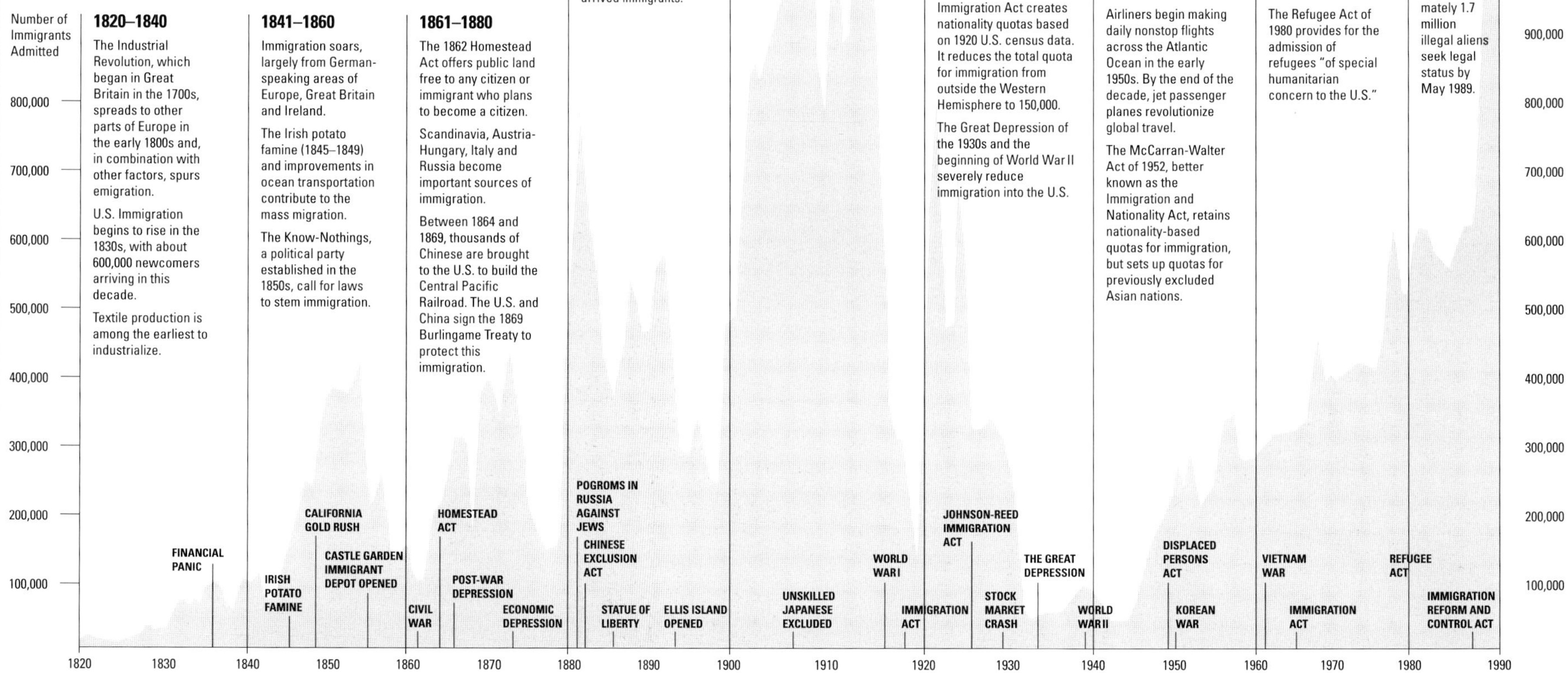

United States Information Agency. *Golden Door: U.S. Immigration and Ellis Island.* Oct. 1990, pp. 4–5.

K. L. Billingsley

Immigration – the American Experience

Although there have been and always will be variations on the American dream, the key component is freedom. Like a magnet drawing iron fillings, America has attracted seekers of liberty from the four corners of the world. Liberated from the oppressive conditions that squashed their talents, the new arrivals could flourish, prosper, and practice their various religions without fear of state reprisal or censure. And along the way something else happened. The new arrivals were transformed, and this is the heart of the American experience.

One would be hard-pressed to find a "Norwegian dream," a Japanese, Russian, Iranian, Nepalese, Pakistani, or Ecuadorian dream. Even an English, German or French dream sounds odd, in spite of the accomplishments of those nations. At home and abroad, the United States is different – an experiment, a new order, a dream.

Immigrants cannot become French, German, or Belgian in the same way they can become Americans. And for most of the nation's history, those who came wanted to become Americans. According to *National Geographic*, the largest public event ever held in New York's Central Park was the 1944 "I am an American Day" celebration, attended by an amazing 2.4 million people. It is hard to think of a similar event in another country.

It is not ethnicity but the adoption of American principles that ultimately makes one an American. The result, as British historian Paul Johnson has noted, is a new and different people, a new character.

Davor Trgovcevic/Kroatien

Tasks:

1. What is – according to Billingsley – the key element of the American dream? Why?
2. What makes people "American?"
3. Now look at the cartoon and describe what you see.
4. Find a suitable caption for the cartoon.
5. What do you know about Superman? Have you seen any Superman films or series?
6. Does this cartoon portray the main thought of the text?
7. Does the cartoon criticize the notion of becoming American? Explain your opinion.

A Survey

A new study of foreign-born adults living in the United States suggests that immigrants are firm believers in the American dream and for most part have received the opportunities needed to achieve it. Although many immigrants retain[1] ties to their homeland through the people they socialize with and the language they speak at home, their commitment to the United States is clear: Immigrants want to remain in the US and most advocate[2] the "melting pot" approach to immigration, with new arrivals encouraged to blend into the American culture.

Lydia Saad and her colleagues at the Gallup Organization conducted the survey[3] from which these findings were taken for *USA Today* and *CNN*. Polling[4] was done June 5–6, 1995, in English only. It therefore represents about three-quarters of the foreign-born population living in the United States. According to US Census Bureau estimates, about one-quarter of all immigrants are not proficient in English, and thus were not able to participate in this telephone survey. Several poll questions suggest that immigrants are unequivocal[5] in the desire to remain in the United States and are enthusiastic about being American. But when asked to compare the United States with their homeland as a place to raise children ambivalence[6] about the American way of life is clearly evident. A bare majority (54%) prefer the United States while one-third say their homeland is the better place.

The vast majority of immigrants – over 80% – do prefer America to their homeland when it comes to the job opportunities available for themselves and their children, and most think the United States superior in terms of legal justice. (...)

Belief in the American dream is nearly universal among immigrants and is higher than in Gallup surveys of the general public. More than nine in ten immigrants (93%) agree that people who work hard to better themselves can get ahead in this country, compared with 85% of all national adults in a survey taken earlier in June. A high proportion of immigrants (70%) also agree that their children will have even better economic opportunities in this country than they have had.

Another major US credential[7] is greater political freedom. Overall, 75% of immigrants say the level of political freedom in the United States is better than what they experienced in their homeland: only 5% say their homeland is better. (...)

The vast majority among all ethnic groups (about 80%) say they felt welcome when they first came to this country. Barely one in ten (9%) say they felt unwelcome. This positive assessment is even higher when immigrants focus on how they feel today; 90% now feel welcome and only 7% unwelcome. (...)

Despite the poll findings suggesting that immigrants maintain strong cultural ties to their homeland, English speaking immigrants clearly favor an approach to immigration which requires blending into the American culture rather than maintaining some important aspects of their original cultures. The so-called multiculturalism effort to preserve ethnic identity is vigorously favored by only 27% of immigrants and 32% of national adults, whereas assimilation is favored by 59% of both immigrants and national adults.

Not only do immigrants prefer the more traditional approach to immigration, but they feel the phrase "melting pot" – people of different cultures blending into a unified American culture – is an accurate description of the United States today. Three-quarters agree with this characterization, while just 20% disagree.

A majority of immigrants hold a more open view of legal immigration than the public at large: 44% prefer keeping immigration at its present level and another 15% want to see it increased. Only one-third of immigrants would like to see legal immigration level in this country decreased. By contrast only one-third of the general public wants legal immigration either expanded or maintained, while two thirds (65%) would like to see it decreased. (...)

Most immigrants who are now citizens, as well as those who still aspire[8] for citizenship, favor the open approach. The "open door" is inherent in the American mystique. Those who passed through it treasure it.

Vocabulary:

1 *to retain* – to keep
2 *to advocate* – to support
3 *survey* – inquiry, questioning
4 *to poll* – to ask people about their opinion
5 *unequivocal* – clear
6 *ambivalence* – both positive and negative
7 *credential* – characteristic
8 *to aspire* – to desire

Tasks:

1. Look up the following words (plus two more of your own choice) and find suitable English definitions or synonyms for them.

l. 2: firm ______

l. 11: to blend ______

l. 19: estimate ______

l. 54: assessment ______

l. 55: to focus ______

l. 61: to favor ______

l. 81: to decrease ______

l. 88: inherent ______

l. ___ ______ ______

l. ___ ______ ______

2. Read the text again and write down the questions the Gallup Organization might have asked. Then copy the percentage/answers given for each question.

questions	*percentage*

3. Summarize – in your own words – the findings of this poll. What does it say about immigration and the American dream today?

4. Surveys such as this should not be discussed uncritically. Try to think of factors which could influence the (relatively positive) outcome of this inquiry.

5. Would you consider emigrating to the US? Why (not)?

Longterm Project:

Make up a fictional person (name – nationality – profession – biography etc.) and have him/her immigrate to the US. Decide when "your immigrant" came to the US (17th–20th century) and where he/she settled. Then, let your fictional immigrant write a letter to friends or the family in his/her homeland, describing the new home, the people, and the experiences made. Was/Is he or she successful and happy? What does he/she like or dislike about the "land of endless opportunity?"

Immigrant Population in U.S. Has Nearly Tripled Since 1970

WASHINGTON – A new study of census[1] data shows that the number of immigrants living in the United States has almost tripled since 1970, rising form 9.6 million to 26.3 million, far outpacing the growth of the native-born population.

The new figures dramatically affirm that the country is going through a remarkable transformation in just one generation, one that will reshape its demographic and social landscape for years to come. As a percentage of the population, immigrants now account for nearly 1 in 10 residents, the highest in seven decades.

The influx[2] of newcomers has transformed communities, whether it is the Bosnians settling in St. Louis, the Russians in northeast Philadelphia, the Dominicans in New York City or the Salvadorans in Silver Spring, Md. Even in places were immigrants have long found a home, the critical mass attained by some groups has made what once was foreign intimately familiar.

Half of the immigrants are also Spanish-speaking – 27% coming from Mexico alone. California, New York and Florida have all seen enormous increases.

The new figures are included in a study conducted by the Center for Immigration Studies here and based on the Census Bureau's Current Population Survey[3] for March 1998.

The study concludes that immigrants accounted for 9.8% of the population, double the 4.8% registered in 1970. Though still considerably lower than the 14.7% attained in 1910, the study concludes that the tide of immigrants entering the country is having a profound, historic effect.

The center, a nonprofit organization that advocates immigration controls, concludes that the overall characteristics of this immigrant pool[4] – poorer, less educated, more inclined to receive welfare – present an "enormous challenge."

Immigration advocates and civil rights groups did not question the numbers but did react to the center's conclusions with skepticism and even concern.

"Sounding the alarm about how many of us there are, are they?", said Cecilia Munoz, vice president for policy at the National Council of La Raza, a Latino civil rights organization. "But it's alarming only if you assume immigrants coming in are harmful to Americans, which they are not."

Los Angeles Times, January 9, 1999

Vocabulary:

1 *census* – Volkszählung
2 *influx* – Zustrom
3 *survey* – Umfrage
4 *immigrant pool* – hier: Anzahl Einwanderer

Tasks:

1. In this text you can find many different verb forms and tenses. Identify the following and explain their use in context.
   l. 8: *is going through* – l. 15: *has transformed* – l. 22: *attained by* – l. 28: *are included* – ll. 47/48: *did react*
2. Summarize the facts given in this text.
3. How would you describe the overall tone of this article? Is the author merely stating the facts or is he conveying an opinion?
4. What do *you* think: Is the increasing number of immigrants in the US a problem?

Bruce Springsteen

Sinaloa Cowboys

Miguel came from a small town in northern Mexico
He came north with his brother Louis
To California three years ago
They crossed at the river levee when Louis was just sixteen
And found work together in the fields of San Joaquin

They left their homes and families
Their father said "My sons one thing you will learn
For everything the north gives it exacts a price in return."
They worked side by side in the orchards
From morning till the day was through
Doing the work the hueros wouldn't do

Word was out some men in from Sinaloa
Were looking for some hands well deep in Fresno county
There was a deserted chicken ranch
There in a small tin shack on the edge of a ravine
Miguel and Louis stood cooking metamphetamine

You could spend a year in the orchards
Or make half as much in one ten-hour shift
Working for the men from Sinaloa
But if you slipped the hydroidic acid
Could burn a hole right through your skin
They'd leave you spitting up blood in the desert
If you breathed those fumes in

It was early one winter evening as Miguel stood watch outside
When the shack exploded, lighting up the valley night
Miguel carried Louis' body over his shoulder down a swale
To the creekside and there in the tall grass Louis Rosales died

Miguel lifted Louis' body into his truck
And then he drove to where the morning sunlight
Fell on a eucalyptus grove
There in the dirt he dug up ten thousand dollars
All that they'd saved; kissed his brother's lips
And placed him in his grave

A 24 Illegal immigration

Miguel came from a small town in northern ________________
He came north with his brother Louis
To California three ________________ ago
They crossed at the river levee[1] when Louis was just ________________
And found work together in the fields of San Joaquin

They left their homes and ________________
Their father said "My sons one thing you will ________________
For everything the north gives it exacts[2] a price in return."
They ________________ side by side in the orchards[3]
From morning till the day was through
Doing the work the hueros wouldn't do

Word was out some men in from Sinaloa
Were ________________ for some hands[4] well deep in Fresno county
There was a deserted ________________ ranch
There in a small tin shack[5] on the edge of a ravine
Miguel and Louis stood ________________ metamphetamine[6]

You could ________________ a year in the orchards
Or make half as much in one ten-hour shift[7]
Working for the men from Sinaloa
But if you ________________ the hydroidic acid[8]
Could burn a hole right through your skin
They'd leave you spitting up blood in the ________________
If you breathed those fumes[9] in

It was early one winter evening as Miguel stood watch[10] ________________
When the shack ________________ lighting up the valley night
Miguel carried Louis' body over his shoulder down a swale[11]
To the creekside and there in the tall grass Louis Rosales ________________

Miguel lifted Louis' body into his truck
And then he drove to where the morning ________________
Fell on a eucalyptus grove[12]
There in the dirt he dug up ten thousand dollars
All that they'd saved; kissed his brother's lips
And placed him in his ________________

1 *levee* – embankment built to protect land from a river in flood
2 *to exact* – to demand
3 *orchard* – piece of ground with fruit trees
4 *hands* – workers
5 *shack* – small hut
6 *metamphetamine* – drug
7 *shift* – period of work
8 *acid* – chemical substance
9 *fumes* – gas
10 *to stand watch* – watching out for possible danger
11 *swale* – shady or sunken spot
12 *grove* – group of trees

Tasks:

1. Listen to the song and write down the words/phrases you understand. Collect them on the board and summarize the bits and pieces of information about the story that are available.
2. Listen to the song again and fill in the missing words on the worksheet.
3. What do you think about the story, the music, the overall atmosphere?
4. Summarize – in your own words – the story of Miguel and Louis.
5. Imagine you are a reporter from a local newspaper. What would your report about this story look like? Keep in mind the journalistic style of such a report.
6. Why, do you think, Springsteen used "Sinaloa Cowboys" as the title of the song?
7. Work in small groups: What will Miguel do now? How will his story continue? Write an appropriate ending and compare it with the others'.
8. Look up California and Mexico in an atlas and try to locate the places mentioned.
9. Read the following information about a proposition in California which has led to major controversies since 1994. (Most of this proposition was ruled unconstitional by a US District Court, which prevented it from taking effect.)

> California initiative making illegal immigrants ineligible for medical care and public school education backed by California governor Pete Wilson and approved by 59 percent of voters in the November 1994 elections. (The San Francisco Bay Area was the only region of the state to reject it.) The day after balloting, enforcement of the law (denying access to prenatal care and nursing homes) was blocked by state and federal courts. In the wake of Prop. 187, discrimination against non-whites has increased and many immigrants won't seek medical help out of fear of deportation. Critics of anti-immigrant legislation contend that illegal immigrants contribute more in taxes than they receive in government services. (A 1994 Urban Institute report put the figures at $ 30 billion and $ 18.7 billion, respectively, estimating that most of the latter goes to refugees from Cold War enemies.)

10. Should illegal aliens receive medical care and be able to attend school? Why (not)?
11. Look up the following words and find synonyms or definitions.

ineligible ______________________________

to back ______________________________

to approve ______________________________

to reject ______________________________

in the wake of ______________________________

to contribute ______________________________

respectively ______________________________

to estimate ______________________________

T. Coraghessan Boyle

The Tortilla Curtain (I)

There was almost no traffic at all at this hour, and that was a pleasant surprise. Darkness clung to the hills, and yet it was mild and the air smelled of the jasmine that trailed from the retaining walls[1] out front of the houses along the road. They walked in silence for an hour, the occasional car stunning[2] them with its headlights before the night crept back in. Things rustled in the brush at the side of the road – mice, she supposed – and twice they heard coyotes howling off in the hills. The moon got bigger as it dipped behind them and América never let the weight of the baby bother her, or its kicks either. She was out of the canyon, away from the spit of sand[3] and that ugly wrecked hulk of a car, and that was all that mattered.

When they reached the top and the San Fernando Valley opened up beneath them like an enormous glittering fan, she had to stop and catch her breath. "Come on," Candído urged, leaning over her as she sat there in a patch of stiff grass, "there's no time to rest." But she'd overestimated herself, and now she felt it: a pregnant woman grown soft in that prison by the stream. Her feet were swollen. She could smell her own sweat. The baby was like a dead weight strapped to the front of her. *"Un momento,"* she whispered, gazing out on the grounded constellations of the Valley floor, grid[4] upon grid of lights, and every one a house, an apartment, a walk-up or flat, every one a promise of a life that would never again be this hard. (...)

Sherman Way. She held the words in her head like a talisman, *Sherman Way*, and then they were moving again, along the black swatch[5] of the road that chased its own tail down the side of the hill. Candído knew the shortcuts, steep narrow trails that plunged through the brush to pinch off the switchbacks[6] at the neck, and he held her hand and helped her through the worst places. Her feet were like stone, clumsy suddenly. Needlegrass stabbed through her dress and things caught at her hair. And now, every time they made the pavement again, there were the cars. It wasn't yet light and already they were there, the first sporadic awakening of that endless stream, roaring up the road opposite them, and there was no joy in that. América kept her head down and skipped along as fast as she could go, eaten up with the fear of *La Migra* and the common accidents at the road.

By the time the sun was up, the ordeal was behind them. They were walking hand in hand up a broad street overhung with trees, a sidewalk beneath their feet, pretty houses with pretty yards stretching as far as they could see. América was exhilarated, on fire with excitement. All the fatigue dropped magically away from her. Clinging to Candído's arm, she peered in at the windows, examined the cars in the driveways and the children's things in the yards with the eye of an appraiser, gave a running commentary on each house as they passed it by. The houses were adorable, *linda, simpática,* cute. That color was striking, didn't he think so? And the bouganvillea – she'd never seen bouganvillea so lush. Candído was mute. His eyes darted everywhere and he looked troubled – he was troubled, worried sick, she knew it, but she couldn't help herself. Oh, look at that one! And that!

They turned next onto a commercial boulevard, the main one in this part of the city, Candído explained, and this was even better. There were shops, wall-to-wall shops, restaurants – was that a Chinese, was that what that writing was? – a supermarket that sprawled out over a lot the size of a *fútbol* stadium with thirty shops more clustered round it. After Tepoztlán, Cuernavaca even, after the Tijuana dump and Venice and the leafy dolorous hell of the canyon, this was a vision of paradise. And when she came to the furniture store – the couches and settees[7] and rugs and elegant lamps all laid out like in the Hollywood movies – Candído couldn't budge[8] her. "Come one, it's getting late, you can look at this junk some

1 *retaining wall* – a wall built to support and confine a mass of earth

2 *to stun* – *here:* to make s.o. unable to see properly for a short time

3 *spit of sand* – small, narrow point of land running out into a body of water

4 *grid* – network of squares

5 *swatch* – pattern

6 *switchbacks* – a mountain road with many sharp bends

7 *settee* – a comfortable seat for two or three people

8 *to budge* – to move sth or sb

other time, come on," he said, tugging at her arm, but she wouldn't move. Not for ten whole minutes. It was almost as if she were in a trance and she didn't care. If she could have done it, she would have moved right into the store and slept on a different couch every night and it wouldn't have bothered her a whit if the whole world was looking in at the window.

T. C. Boyle: English professor in the creative writing program at the University of Southern California – he has written six novels and four collections of short stories so far.

Tasks:

1. Find a substitute which fits this context.

   l. 16: ... gazing out on – ______________________________

   ll. 22/23: ... trails that plunged through the brush – ______________________________

   l. 38: That color was striking – ______________________________

   ll. 39/40: His eyes darted everywhere – ______________________________

   l. 47: ... the leafy dolorous hell of the canyon – ______________________________

2. Gather the information you can collect from this excerpt (who, what, where, when). Then give a short summary.

time and place	about América	about Candído

3. Find a suitable title for this excerpt.
4. Why do you think is Candído so afraid when they come into the city?
5. The novel is entitled *"The Tortilla Curtain;"* what does this metaphor refer to?
6. Can you identify the following stylistic/rhetorical devices?

   l. 2: Darkness clung to the hills – ______________________________

   l. 5: ... rustled in the brush – ______________________________

   ll. 10/11: ... San Fernando Valley opened up like an enormous glittering fan – ______________________________

   ____

l. 20: Sherman Way … Sherman Way – ______________________________

l. 38: … adorable, *linda, simpática,* cute – ______________________________

ll. 47/48: … hell … paradise – ______________________________

7. Having only read this short passage, would you want to read the novel? Why (not)?
8. Locate the San Ferndando Valley on a map. Try to gather some information about California and present it to the class.

T. Coraghessan Boyle

The Tortilla Curtain (II)

"Okay, buckaroo[1]," he called over his shoulder, "you've got two choices today as far as your hi-fiber[2] bar[3] is concerned: Cranberry Nut or Boysenberry Supreme. What'll it be?",

(…)

Jordan reached up with his left hand, as Delaney knew he would fastening on the Boysenberry Supreme bar just as Kyra, hunched over the weight of two boxes of hand-addressed envelopes – Excelsior, 500 Count – clattered into the kitchen in her heels. She made separate kissing motions in the direction of her husband and son, then slid into her chair, poured herself half a cup of coffee lightened with skim milk[4] – for the calcium – and began sifting purposively through the envelopes.

"Why can't I have Sugar Pops or Honey Nut Cheerios like other kids? Or bacon and eggs?", Jordan pinched his voice. "Mom? Why can't I?"

Kyra gave the stock response – "You're not other kids, that's why" – and Delaney was taken back to his own childhood, a rainy night in the middle of an interminable winter, a plate of liver, onions and boiled potatoes before him.

"I hate granola," Jordan countered, and it was like a Noh Play[5], timeless ritual.

"It's good for you."

"Yeah, sure." Jordan made an exaggerated slurping sound, sucking the milk through his teeth.

"Think of all the little children who have nothing to eat," Kyra said without looking up, and Jordan, sticking to the script, came right back at her: "Let's send them this."

Now she looked up. "Eat," she said, and the drama was over.

"Busy day?", Delaney murmured, setting Kyra's orange juice down beside the newspaper and unscrewing the childproof caps of the sturdy plastic containers that held her twelve separate vitamin and mineral supplements. He did little things for her – out of love and consideration, sure, but also in acknowledgement of the fact that she was the chief breadwinner here, the one who went off to the office while he stayed home. Which was all right by him. He had none of those juvenile macho hang-ups[6] about role reversal and who wore the pants and all of that – real estate was her life, and he was more than happy to help her with it, so long as he got his four hours a day at the keyboard.

1 *buckaroo* – cowboy
2 *hi-fiber* – high percentage of those parts of the grain which are indigestible
3 *bar* – block of solid material i.e. chocolate
4 *skim milk* – milk from which the cream has been removed (= low-fat)
5 *Noh Play* – traditional Japanese style of drama
6 *hang-up* – a problem about which someone is obsessed

Tasks:

1. Look up the unknown words you consider important.
2. Write two short paragraphs describing Delaney and Kyra. What do you think of them?
3. Try to imagine what their everyday life looks like – their house, their meals, their friends.
4. What kind of job could allow Delaney to spend "four hours a day at the keyboard?"
5. It's early evening: Write a small scene with the three of them having dinner.
6. Read this excerpt from a book review in which the author criticizes Boyle's portrayal of Delaney and Kyra Mossbacher. What danger does Spencer see in Boyle's contempt for the Mossbachers? Do you agree?

> "Mr. Boyle's fictional strategy is puzzling. Why are we being asked to follow the fates of characters for whom he clearly feels such contempt? (...)
> Yet, where the socially engaged novel once offered critique, Mr. Boyle provides contempt...
> Contempt causes us to jeer rather than speak, to poke rather than touch."
>
> Scott Spencer, The New York Times Book Review 1995

7. In these two excerpts from "The Tortilla Curtain" you have been introduced to the main characters. Think of situations/events in which the lives of Candído, América, Delaney, and Kyra could collide.

Picture Press, CORBIS, Hamburg

American-Mexican border

CHINA
Dienbienphu
Hanoi
Haiphong
GULF OF TONKIN
U.S. BOMBING HALT MARCH 1968
LAOS
NORTH VIETNAM
Vientiane
U.S. BOMBING HALT NOVEMBER 1968
DEMILITARIZED ZONE
Khe Sanh
Quang Tri
THAILAND
Hué
Danang
Mekong River
Korat
My Lai
Dak To
Quang Ngai
Kontum
An Khe
Pleiku
Bangkok
Qui Nhon
CAMBODIA
TET OFFENSIVE 1968
CENTRAL HIGHLANDS
NhaTrang
Cam Ranh Bay
SOUTH VIETNAM
Bo Duc
Ben Cat
1970
1970
Pnompenh
Bien Hoa
Saigon
Dong Tam
MEKONG DELTA
Can Tho
GULF OF SIAM
Soc Trang
SOUTH CHINA SEA
THE WAR IN VIETNAM
United States and South Vietnamese troop moves
National Liberation Army moves
Capitol cities
Major U.S. Bases
0
100 MILES

1930:	Indochinese Communist Party, opposed to French rule, organized by Ho Chi Minh and his followers.
1945:	An OSS (Office of Strategic Services, forerunner of the CIA) team parachutes into Ho Chi Minh's jungle camp in northern Vietnam and saves Ho Chi Minh who is ill with malaria and other tropical diseases.
August, 1945:	Japan surrenders. Ho Chi Minh establishes the Viet Minh, a guerilla army. Bao Dai abdicates after a general uprising.
September 2, 1945:	Ho Chi Minh reads Vietnam's Declaration of Independence and establishes the Democratic Republic of Vietnam in Hanoi. Vietnam is divided.
August 3, 1950:	A U.S. Military Assistance Advisory Group (MAAG) of 35 men arrives in Saigon. By the end of the year, the U.S. is bearing half of the cost of France's war effort in Vietnam.
June, 1954:	The CIA establishes a military mission in Saigon. Bao Dai selects Ngo Dinh Diem as prime minister of his government.
1955:	The U.S.-backed Ngo Dinh Diem organizes the Republic of Vietnam as an independent nation and declares himself president.
July 8, 1959:	The first American combat death in Vietnam occurs.
1960:	The National Liberation Front (NLF) – called the Viet Cong – is founded in South Vietnam.
November 1, 1963:	South Vietnamese President Diem is assassinated.
August 2 and 4, 1964:	The Gulf of Tonkin Incident. North Vietnamese torpedo boats attacked the U.S. destroyer Maddox in the Gulf of Tonkin. A second attack allegedly occurs on August 4 – August 7, 1964: Congress approves the Gulf of Tonkin Resolution which allows the president to take any necessary measures to repel further attacks and to provide military assistance to any SEATO member. President Johnson orders the bombing of North Vietnam.
March 8, 1965:	First U.S. combat troops reach South Vietnam.
September, 1967:	Thieu is elected president of South Vietnam.
Oct. 21–23, 1967:	50,000 people demonstrate against the war in Washington, D.C.
January 21, 1968:	The battle of Khe Sanh begins, ending six months later.
January 31, 1968:	The Tet Offensive: North Vietnamese troops attack Saigon and other major cities inflicting heavy casualties on U.S. soldiers.
March 16, 1968:	The My Lai massacre: U.S. platoon under Lt. W. Calley massacre more than 300 South Vietnamese villagers.
May 20, 1969:	The Paris peace talks begin. – July 8, 1969: President Richard Nixon announces the first troop withdrawals from South Vietnam.
September 3, 1969:	Ho Chi Minh dies.
November 15, 1969:	250,000 people demonstrate against the war in Washington D.C.
April 30, 1970:	The armies of the U.S. and South Vietnam invade Cambodia.
May 4, 1970:	Four students are killed by National Guardsmen at Kent State University in Ohio while protesting against the invasion of Cambodia. – May 6, 1970: More than 100 colleges are closed due to student riots over Kent State.
February, 1971:	Laos is invaded – December, 1972: Christmas bombing of Hanoi
January 27, 1973:	The United States and North Vietnam sign Paris Peace Accords, ending American combat role in war. U.S. military draft ends.
March 29, 1973:	Last U.S. combat troops leave Vietnam. – February 12–27, 1973: POWs (= Prisoners of War) begin to come home as part of Operation Homecoming.
April 1, 1973:	Hanoi releases last 591 acknowledged American POWs.
April 29, 1975:	Saigon falls; last Americans evacuated; last American combat death
April 30, 1975:	North Vietnamese forces take over Saigon, South Vietnam surrenders to North Vietnam, ending the war and reunifying the country under communist control. Washington extends embargo to all of Vietnam.
April 10, 1997:	Former POW Douglas "Pete" Peterson is confirmed by the Senate as the first ambassador to Vietnam since the end of the war and the first ever to be posted to Hanoi. Vietnam's Le Van Bang is confirmed as Vietnam's ambassador to the United States.

http://servercc.oakton.edu/~wittman/

Jefferey L. Turk, Sr.

The Dreams are Back

The Dreams are back.
You know the dreams –
Where there is no escape
I run, and run, and run
nowhere to run –
nowhere to hide –
no going home.

The Dreams are back.
The Dreams … my friends, the Dreams.
At least in the Dreams
I can run
I am not stuck on four legs …
or wheels …
The Dreams can be my friends.

The Dreams are back.
I fight the enemy –
I kick, I hit, I claw!
To wake and find my first wife
or my second
or my girlfriend
unconscious and bleeding.

The Dreams are back.
In the Dreams I know who I am
and who you are.
I am not surrounded by those
whose priorities are new cars
or getting laid –
but staying alive.

The Dreams are back.
I thought I'd left the Dreams behind.
Six months without the Dreams.
Six months of drug-induced slumber,
Six months of thinking
I was healed
The Dreams are back.

The Dreams are back.
The Dreams are back.
The Dreams are back.
The Dreams are back.
The Dreams are back.
The Dreams are back.
THE DREAMS ARE BACK!

http://grunt.space.swri.edu/dreambak.htm

____________________ are back.

You know ____________________
Where there is no escape
I run, and run, and run
no where to run –
nowhere to hide –
no going home.

____________________ are back.

____________________ my friends, ____________________.
At least in ____________________
I can run
I am not stuck on four legs …
or wheels …
____________________ can be my friends.

Tasks:

1. *(= Pre-reading activity)* Work with your neighbor and fill in the blanks. You can either use the same or different words in all the blanks.
2. *(= Pre-reading activity)* Read the two stanzas aloud and explain your choice of words.
3. *(= Pre-reading activity)* Work in groups of two to four:
   Find adjectives to describe the atmosphere in this poem.
   Try to put them together in groups (i.e. negative/positive connotations).
   Compare your clusters with the others'.
4. Now look at the original; how does it differ from your version? What do you think of it?
5. Take three minutes and quickly write down anything that comes to mind when you think of the word "dream:"

   ____

   ____

   ____

   Compare and discuss your list with your neighbor and present in class the words you have in common.

Lori M. E. Gilbertson

After After

I was your princess
dreamy prom queen
as far as I could figure it was me
it was me and
I would heal your screams
when you cried at night
when you covered your head
and hid in the brush,
with unmentioned enemies,
dismembered friends
then woke in the morning to poke
holes in my head with a black fit, a white fit
that made no goddamned sense.
No turning, no twisting could make it all clear
when you screamed in your sleep and
covered your head

and woke in the morning,
a smile and a wink to tell
of a woman, the soldier, the spy
the hideous form, the beautiful eyes,
rifle, her hands;
life tucked inside;
so proud of yourself that's what you said
not just one
not just one
but two, two you said
the first that you killed
slap on the back:
"a young boy like you will do fucking fine"
and you hid your eyes
a smile that scarred.

and I cried in the night while you
rocked in your sleep
and I tried,
I tried,
but you turned,
you turned on me
"Charlie, Charlie"
you screamed and you screamed
something about Cong
nothing about fright,
the end of us all
but it was me
it was me
IT WAS ME
not Charlie,
the night your mind burst apart.

Tasks:

6. Read through the poem. Explain the word "prom." What is a (white/black) "fit?" Who is "Charlie?"
7. Summarize (in your own words) the behavior of the man in "After After." What does he do? How does he act?
8. Pick three of the following nouns which – in your opinion – come closest to the central messages of these two poems. Can you think of other possibilities?
   memory – confusion – ghosts – pity – tension – rage – struggle – despair – conscience – pain – cruelty
9. Work with your partner. Compare this poem to *"The Dreams are Back;"* which similarities and differences can you find? Put together a list and discuss your findings in class.
10. Which one of the poems do you like better? Why?
11. Project: Form groups and think of ways how to "stage" one of the poems: You could present it either personally on stage or make a tape; you could add music or pictures, have actors or "background vocals" … use your imagination!

In Memoriam: Vietnam

Impressions from the Vietnam Memorial in Washington D. C.

Visitors began leaving tokens of remembrance at the Vietnam Veterans Memorial in 1982, while it was still under construction. Flags and flowers historically have decorated veterans' monuments, but the presence of many other mementos is unique to the Vietnam Veterans Memorial. The first, a Purple Heart, was thrown by a Vietnam veteran into the wet cement of the Memorial's foundation.

Since then, visitors from at home and abroad have left more than 25,000 keepsakes at the Memorial, collected daily by National Park Service rangers. They express the love, grief, and pain the visitors associate with the 58,183 names on the Memorial's 140 black granite panels.

This unsolicited outpouring occurs year round, particularly at Christmas, Memorial Day, July 4th, and Veterans Day. The gifts also commemorate birthdays of dead and missing veterans and other days of personal importance. This selection of remembrances provides us an opportunity to ponder the continuing impact of the Vietnam Veterans Memorial on the generation that lived through that conflict.

Introduction to "Personal Legacy. The Healing of a Nation"
A joint exhibition of the National Museum of American History, the Smithsonian Institution and the National Park Service.

Picture Press, CORBIS, Hamburg

Picture Press, CORBIS, Hamburg

Ron Kovic

Born on the Fourth of July (I)

In the last month of school, the marine recruiters came and spoke to my senior class. They marched both in perfect step, into the auditorium with their dress blue uniforms and their magnificently shined shoes. It was like all the movies and all the books and all the dreams of becoming a hero come true. (...)

"Good afternoon, men," the tall marine said, "We have come today because they told us that some of you want to become marines." He told us that the marines took nothing but the best, that if any of us did not think we were good enough, we should not even think of joining. The tall marine spoke in a very beautiful way about the exciting history of the marines and how they had never lost and America had never been defeated.

"The marines have been the first in everything, first to fight and first to uphold the honor of our country. We have served on distant shores and at home, and we have always come when our country has called. There is nothing finer, nothing prouder, than a United States Marine."

When they were finished, they efficiently picked up their papers and marched together down the steps of the stage to where a small crowd of boys began to gather. I couldn't wait to run down after them, meet with them and shake their hands. And as I shook their hands and stared up into their eyes, I couldn't help but feel I was shaking hands with John Wayne and Audie Murphy. They told us that day that the Marine Corps built men – body, mind, and spirit. And that we could serve our country like the young president had asked us to do.

We were all going in different directions and we had our whole lives ahead of us, and a million different dreams. I can still remember the last stickball game. I stood at home plate with the sun in my face and looked out at Richie, Pete, and the rest. It was our last summer together and the last stickball game we ever played on Hamilton Avenue.

One day that summer, I quit my job at the food store and went to the little red, white, and blue shack in Levittown. My father and I went down together. It was September by the time all the paperwork was completed, September 1964. I was going to leave on a train one morning and become a marine.

I stayed up most of the night before I left, watching the late movie. Then "The Star-Spangled Banner" played. I remember standing up and feeling very patriotic, chills running up and down my spine. I put my hand over my heart and stood rigid at attention until the screen went blank.

Tasks:

1. Practise reading the text aloud. Pay special attention to pronunciation and intonation. Read slow enough so listeners without a text can follow.
2. Choose three words which are likely to be unknown to some of the students and look them up in a dictionary. Explain the words by using examples or synonyms.
3. Try to find three synonyms (or words with a similar meaning) for "magnificent," (l. 3) which would fit here.
4. Decide on *one* sentence in this text you consider representative of the narrator's attitude. Explain your choice.
5. This kind of patriotism might be difficult to understand today. What about the early sixties? Do you know anything about this period of time, which would help explain Kovic' attitude?
6. If you had only read this short passage, would you want to read the whole book? Why (not)?

Ron Kovic

Born on the Fourth of July (II)

What kind of miserable life was this, no friends, no legs, people staring at him wherever he went. The depression sometimes was awesome, like he was drowning in it, and no matter how hard he tried he wasn't ever getting out. He had even sometimes invented things that weren't true, made believe so the feelings would go away. But now he wasn't making things up anymore, he was too tired to do that, in too much pain. Where were his legs that used to run? he thought.

He wanted people around. He wanted someone to call him on the phone. He wanted just one friend he could talk to about the real things, the painful truths about his miserable existence that would make most people walk away from him – "Sorry I gotta run now. I'm late already." (...)

He had been born on the Fourth of July, he had been their Yankee Doodle Dandy, their all-American boy. He had given them almost his whole being in the war and now, after all that, they weren't satisfied with three-quarters being gone, they wanted to take the rest of him. It was crazy but he knew that's what they wanted. They wanted his head and his mind, the numb legs and the wheelchair, they wanted everything. It had all been one big dirty trick and he didn't know what to think anymore. All he had tried to do was tell the truth about the war. But now he just wanted it to be quiet, to be where they weren't cursing at him and beating him and jailing him, lying and calling him a traitor. He had never been anything but a thing to them, a thing to put a uniform on and train to kill, a young thing to run through the meat-grinder, a cheap small nothing to make mincemeat out of.

And somewhere along the way he had forgotten to be polite anymore, and how to be a nice person. Somewhere through it all they had taken even that and he wanted it back so much, so very desperately, he would give almost anything to be able to be kind to people again, but the big machine, the one that had given him the number and the rifle, had sucked it all out of him forever.

They had made him confused and uncertain and blind with hate. They wanted to make him hide like he was hiding now. How many more, he thought, how many more like him were out there hiding in a thousand other Hurricane Streets? He was a living reminder of something terrible and awful.

from: Kovic, Ron. *Born on the Fourth of July.* Simon & Schuster/Pocket Books: New York 1977.

Tasks:

1. Practise reading the text aloud. Pay special attention to pronunciation and intonation. Read slow enough so listeners without a text can follow.
2. Choose three words which are likely to be unknown to some of the students and look them up in a dictionary. Explain the words by using examples or synonyms.
3. Try to find three synonyms (or words with similar meaning) for "awesome," (l. 2) which would fit here.
4. Decide on *one* sentence in this text you consider representative of the narrator's attitude. Explain your choice.
5. Why do you think is this text written in the third person even though the author is talking about himself? Wouldn't the first person be more suitable?
6. If you had only read this short passage, would you want to read the whole book? Why (not)?

Bruce Springsteen

Born in the U.S.A. (1984)

Born down in a dead man's town
The first kick I took was when I hit the ground
You end up like a dog that's been beat too much
Till you spend half your life just covering up

(chorus:)
Born in the U.S.A.
I was born in the U.S.A.
I was born in the U.S.A.
Born in the U.S.A.

Got in a little hometown jam[1]
so they put a rifle in my hand
Sent me off to a foreign land
to go and kill the yellow man

Born in the U.S.A.
I was born in the U.S.A.
I was born in the U.S.A.
Born in the U.S.A.

Come back home to the refinery[2]
Hiring man says: "Son, if it was up to me ..."
Went down to see my V.A.[3] man
He said: "Son, don't you understand, now"

Had a brother at Khe Sanh[4]
fighting off the Vietcong
They're still there, he's all gone
He had a woman he loved in Saigon
I got a picture of him in her arms, now

Down the shadow of the penitentiary[5]
Out by the gas fires of the refinery
I'm ten years burning down the road
Nowhere to run, ain't got nowhere to go

Born in the U.S.A.
I was born in the U.S.A.
I was born in the U.S.A.
Born in the U.S.A.
I'm a long gone daddy in the U.S.A.
Born in the U.S.A.
Born in the U.S.A.
Born in the U.S.A.
I'm a cool rocking daddy in the U.S.A.

Vocabulary:

1 *hometown jam* – small criminal offense: When caught, the "criminal" (in the 60's) often could choose between going to prison or joining the army.
2 *refinery* – factory
3 *V.A. = Veterans' Affairs* – government organization which administers the laws providing benefits and other services to war veterans and their dependents, including medical care, benefits, social support.
4 *Khe Sanh* – location of a US Marine base. In 1967, it was involved in severe fighting and many soldiers were killed.
5 *penitentiary* – prison

The Vietnam War (1946–1975): In 1954, the Americans became involved when they decided to support South Vietnam against the Communist north. In 1957, the Vietcong (South-Vietnamese Communists and enemies of the US-supported government) started their fight. With support from North Vietnam, the Vietcong formed the National Liberation Front of South Vietnam (NLF). By 1968, over 500,000 American troops helped the South Vietnamese to fight the Vietcong. Finally, in 1973, a peace treaty was signed by the US, North and South Vietnam and the US withdrew all their military by the end of 1973.

In 1975, Saigon fell and the North Vietnamese won the war against the South. In 1976, South and North Vietnam were re-united and became the "Socialist Republic of Vietnam". The US lost nearly 60,000 soldiers and many veterans who returned were not able to adjust to normal life again. Many couldn't keep their jobs, committed suicide, took drugs or turned criminal, because the brutal jungle war had destroyed their belief in their country and justice. Even today, the Vietnam War continues to haunt the American psyche – as numerous movies and books have shown.

Tasks:

1. Listen to the song and draw your first impressions (sketches need not be of professional quality!!!). Describe your impressions with the help of your picture.
2. Now, watch the video and pay special attention to the images Springsteen uses in his concert performance. Try to find as many as possible.

____

____

____

3. Compare your pictures with the ones in the video. Are they similar or do they differ?
4. The flag is a powerful image – where does it appear in this video? What does it symbolize – particularly at the end of the video? Work with your neighbor and present your opinion in class.
5. Which emotions are conveyed through music and pictures? Explain.

____

6. Work with your neighbor. Look at the lyrics and summarize the text in your own words.
7. Compare pictures, music, and text: Do the lyrics convey a different message?
8. Do you like the song? Why (not)? Write a short review of it.
9. Look at the following list and cross out the words that do not fit.

   upset – angry – furious – enraged – merry – annoyed – irritated – buoyant – aggravated – incensed – jovial – infuriated – berserk – irascible – displeased – exhilarated – rancorous – grudging – livid – radiant – frenzied

10. Try to put the remaining words into one of the columns below. Work with your neighbor.

a little angry	rather angry	extremely angry

11. Work in small groups. Make the song's character come alive by giving him a name and a history. Present him in class.
12. Project: Imagine the man decides to kill himself and writes his farewell letter to explain his suicide.

Archibald MacLeish

The Unimagined America

The whole history of our continent is a history of the imagination. Men imagined land beyond the sea and found it. No force of terror, no pressure of population, drove our ancestors across this continent. They came, as the great explorers crossed the Atlantic, because of the imagination of the minds – because they imagined a better, a more beautiful, a freer, a happier world; because they were men not only of courage, not only of strength and hardiness, but of warm and vivid desire; because they desired; because they had the power to desire.

And what was true of the continent was true of the Republic. Because our forefathers were able to conceive a free man's government, they were able to create it. Because those who lived before us in this nation were able to imagine a new thing, a thing unheard of in the world before, a thing the sceptical and tired men who did not trust in dreams had not been able to imagine, they erected on this continent the first society in which mankind was to be free, all mankind.

The courage of the Declaration of Independence is far greater than the bravery of those who risked their necks to sign it. The courage of the Declaration of Independence is the courage of the act of imagination. Jefferson's document is an image of a life, a plan of life, a dream – indeed a dream. (...)

When we speak of destiny today, we speak still in terms of the agricultural and sparsely settled nation Thomas Jefferson and his contemporaries had in mind.(...)

This, and not the world beyond us, is the world we turn to: the lost, nostalgic image of a world that was the future to a generation dead a hundred years. No other image has been made to take its place. No one had dreamed a new American dream of the new America – the industrial nation of the huge machines, the limitless earth, the vast and skillful population, the mountains of copper and iron, the mile-long plants, the delicate laboratories, the tremendous dams. (...)

Is it inconceivable that men should achieve a life with the machines as disciplined and honorable and as free as the life that Jefferson believed they could achieve with mules and oxen? Is it certain that the human spirit can survive and flourish only in a world where need and hardship drive with stinging whips?

Is the fault within the machines or with ourselves? Is it because we have automobiles to ride in, because we can purchase certain commodities easily, because our presses can turn out tons of printed paper in a day, that our fiber is soft, our will feeble, our suggestibility infantile? Or is it because we do not use these things as we should use them – because we have not made them serve our moral purpose as a people, but only our private comfort? (...)

A hundred and fifty years ago de Crèvecœur asked a famous question which echoes now: "What then is the American, this new man?". But what then *is* he? What then is he now? A man incapable of the act of the imagination, or a man to whom it is native and natural? A man to dare the dream of plenty with all its risks and dangers, or a man to hold the old nostalgic landscape with the simple virtues safely forced upon him by the necessary self-denial?

Which of these two men is the American? A while ago we should have said the American character was self-evident: a restless man, a great builder and maker and shaper... an inveterate voyager and changer and finder. A man naturally hopeful; a believing man, believing that things progress, that things get forwarder.... A man of certain unquestioned convictions – of a strong, natural attachment to certain ideas and to certain ideals. (...)

We should have said the principal characteristic of the American people was a confidence in the future and themselves – confidence that the future was the thing they'd make it. (...)

I cannot believe we have so changed that we do not believe in ourselves and the future.

And yet we have not done what must be done if we believe the future is the thing we'll make it. We have not named that future.

Archibald MacLeish (1892–1982): American poet, social critic, and professor – supported F. D. Roosevelt's *New Deal* – director of the Library of Congress (1939–44) – rhetoric professor at Harvard University and Amherst College – received the Pulitzer Prize for poetry (1933 and 1953) and for drama (1959), as well as the National Book Award (1953) – "The Unimagined America" was published in 1943.

Tasks:

1. Take a few minutes to read through the whole text. Look up the unknown words and write down ten that you consider important and would like to learn. Discuss your choice in class.
2. Now read through each paragraph again and find a suitable heading/title for it.

   ll. 1–21: ______________________________

   ll. 22–31: ______________________________

   ll. 32–41: ______________________________

   ll. 42–48: ______________________________

   ll. 49–57: ______________________________

   ll. 58–76: ______________________________

   ll. 77–85: ______________________________

3. The author of this text uses several stylistic/rhetorical devices. Find at least one example for each of the following ones and explain what effect they have on the reader.
   a) *accumulation* = stringing together of words with similar meaning
   b) *anaphora* = repeating the same expression at the beginning of sentences with similar structure.
   c) *amplification* = repeating of words and expressions
   d) *contrast* = expressing ideas with opposite meaning within one sentence or adjoining sentences.
   e) *rhetorical question* = a question in form, not requiring an answer, because the answer is already implied
4. Because of the frequent use of rhetorical devices this text is suitable for reading aloud. Practise reading one paragraph with your neighbor and then try to read it in class. Imagine it is a speech; pay special attention to intonation, stress, speed, and pauses.
5. Summarize in your own words the most important points in MacLeish's text.
6. Does the author delineate a positive picture of the American people?
7. Do you agree with his characterization?
8. Which of the key terms and ideas about the American dream are mentioned or described here?
9. Discuss what MacLeish might mean with the last sentence: "We have not named that future."

Crossword Puzzle

Many of the words in this crossword have to do with the "American dream" – some shorter ones are more general. Work with your neighbor.

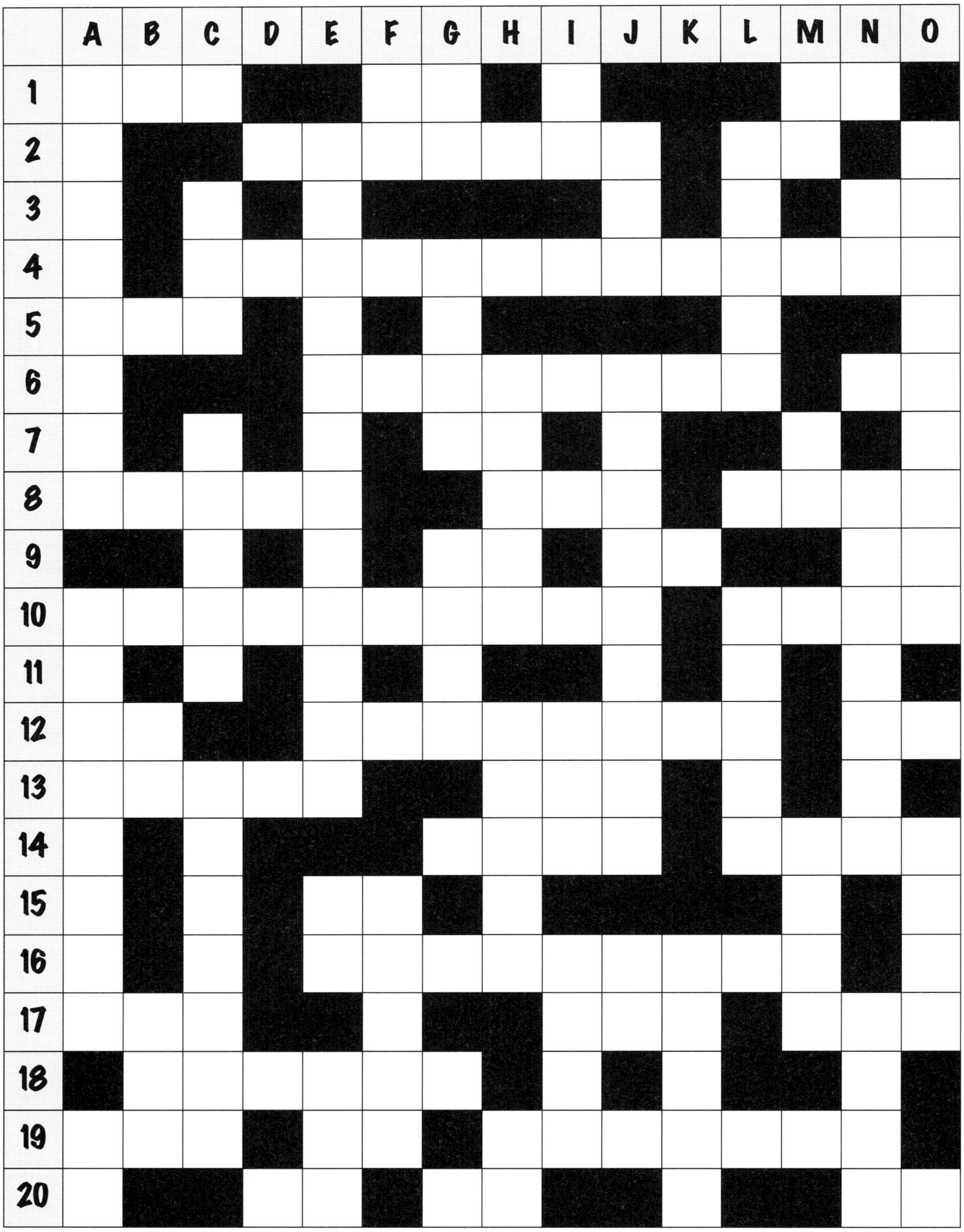

Crossword – Questions

Horizontal (→):

A1: In this the new American people should be melted
F1: Abbreviation for "Alcoholics Anonymous"
M1: Here the first settlers founded Jamestown *(short form)*
D2: Very important person in the Civil War era
L2: Spielberg's most famous alien
N3: Indicating morning hours
C4: Central trait in the American dream
A5: Looks like a mouse, only bigger
E6: They were the first at Plymouth Rock
N6: For example *(abbreviation)*
G7: Popular American hospital TV series *(abbreviation)*
A8: Spot of dirt on clothing
H8: Anti-lock breaking system *(abbreviation)*
L8: She wrote "The New Colossus" (first name)
G9: Nearly every household has at least one
J9: The "Sunshine State" *(abbreviation)*
A10: He was French, but he wrote as an "American Farmer"
L10: The frontier moved this way
A12: Short form for "Lieutenant"
E12: Claimed to have discovered India
N12: Personal pronoun
A13: Major figure in the Enlightenment
H13: What you do with your eyes
G14: A sum of money available for certain causes
L14: Fathers and …
E15: Preposition
E16: To pursue this is granted in the Constitution
A17: Weekday *(abbreviation)*
I17: Short form for another military rank
M17: Black stuff – sticky, fluid, and smelly when hot
B18: The biggest celebration day in July
A19: "Once and for …" (= now and for the only or last time)
E19: Short form for "New York"
H19: They received their name due to Columbus' mistake
D20: This state's capital is Atlanta *(short form)*
G20: United States *(abbreviation)*
N20: Conjunction

Vertical (↓):

A1: The process of improvement
A10: Another term for "universities"
A19: President Clinton's home state *(short form)*
B17: American Federation of Labor *(abbreviation)*
C3: Very prestigious institute in Massachusetts
C7: Literary word for "safe place"
C13: This building is as famous as the White House
E2: This is what America declared 1776
E15: Columbus is this state's capital *(short form)*
F1: Indefinite article
F15: Main character in Cooper's "Leatherstocking Tales"
G1: Americans turn that on when it gets too hot *(abbreviation)*
G4: Another word for "disgusting" or "shameful"
G9: To do very hard physical work
H6: The last place of rest
H12: To wrongfully take sb's position of authority (i.e. throne)
H19: Form of "to be"
I1: First name of Clinton's Vice-President
I12: "All … are created equal"
I16: Symbolic image
J2: State University in New York *(abbreviation)*
J6: Lazarus' poem is … on a plate
J16: Abbreviation of "number"
K16: The King of Rock'n' Roll
L2: This island was the doorway to the US
L10: Short form for "White Anglo-Saxon Males"
M1: Montpelier is the capital of this small state *(short form)*
M7: Indicating afternoon or evening hours
M14: To force sb to leave his position
N3: Conjunction
N8: Manifest destiny symbolizes the United States' … to democratize the world
N17: Another word for "too"
O2: Person who comes to another country to live there
O14: A famous actor or actress

America's Legacy

1. Describe the cartoon and speculate on what "Lady Liberty" is passing on.

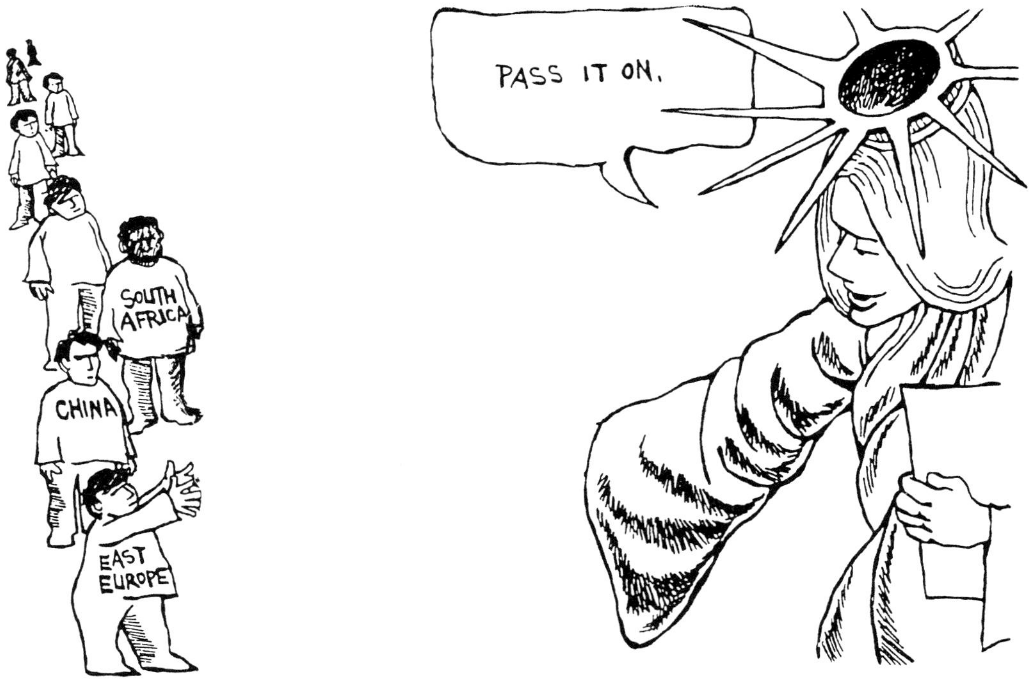

Boileau Frankfort State Journal 90 Rothco

2. Now look at the complete drawing and compare it with your suggestions.
3. Summarize the main idea behind this cartoon.
4. In which way is it related to the American dream?
5. Put something else into the hand of "Lady Liberty" in order to change the meaning of the cartoon. Present your version in class.

Boileau Frankfort State Journal 90 Rothco

A SUBTLE FORM OF DISSENT

New world; new sorts of anti-Americanism

BY JONATHAN FREEDLAND

The old, crude anti-Americanism is fading. With the cold war over, the left has felt able to drop its Vietnam-era obligation to side against Uncle Sam. Now center-left governments from London to Rome to Jerusalem wear their American influence with pride. I welcome this shift. But it would be a mistake to trade the previous blanket[1] condemnation of the United States for an equally undiscriminating embrace of it. For there are some aspects of American conduct that we have every right to abhor[2]. In the globalized 21st century, we have more than a right; we have a duty to turn to America every now and again and just say no.

In the past, anti-Americans saved their bile[3] for two separate areas of U.S. misconduct. They were appalled, first, by America's antics[4] abroad. They were disgusted, second, by the way Americans behaved inside their own country. Intellectuals would inveigh against[5] a society apparently riddled with[6] crime, riven by[7] race and obsessed with money. Now, thanks to globalization, the two older forms of hostility have converged: America's external and internal conduct have become one and the same thing. Now it's not nuclear warheads or the CIA that anti-Americans fear, but what the United States does to itself. For, in today's world, that affects people far beyond America's shores.

If America cultivates genetically modified foods, then green activists in Australia will be justifiably concerned: the risk to the environment is disrespectful of borders. And if Americans' cultural habits change, then so do ours: what "they" watch in Kansas is what "we" watch in Kazakhstan. The old anti-Americanism, which had foreigners sneering at the Yanks, must give way to a subtler form of dissent. The rest of the world now has a legitimate stake in faulting[8] the way Americans live their own lives. For in the new century, what happens in the United States happens to all of us.

FREEDLAND *is a columnist for The Guardian and the author of "Bring Home the Revolution" (4th Estate, London).*

Vocabulary:

1 *blanket* – applying generally
2 *to abhor* – verabscheuen
3 *bile* – *here:* wrath, anger
4 *antic* – trick, strange action
5 *to inveigh against* – *hier:* sich vehement gegen etw. wenden
6 *riddled with* – zerfressen von
7 *riven by* – gespalten
8 *to fault* – to censure, to criticize

Tasks:

1. What has changed – according to Freedland – and why?
2. Which two areas did anti-Americans criticize in the past? What has happened to these two areas?
3. Why is it legitimate for other countries to oppose the United States' national actions or decisions?
4. Summarize in your own words what Freedland means with "a subtle form of dissent."
5. Do you agree? How would you describe and judge the role the US play on a global level today? Which role does America play for Germany?

Vorwort

Der Begriff *American dream* ist ein Schlüsselkonzept zum Verständnis der amerikanischen Gesellschaft. In diesem Traum vereinen sich Vorstellungen, die die Lebenswirklichkeit der „Neuen Welt“ bis heute entscheidend prägen und die auch die Vorstellungen von Generationen von Einwanderern bestimmt haben. Begriffe wie Gleichheit, Unabhängigkeit, Freiheit, Fortschritt und materieller Erfolg bilden die zentralen Bestandteile dieses Traums.
Dieser Glaube an Amerika als das *Promised Land* verstärkt auch die Niederlagen und Krisen der amerikanischen Gesellschaft und lässt diese noch krasser hervortreten. Nur vor dem Hintergrund des *American dream* kann man wirklich verstehen, wie nachhaltig Ereignisse wie der Vietnam-Krieg oder die Morde an den Kennedys und Martin Luther King die Gesellschaft der USA prägen. Auch die andauernde Diskriminierung von Minderheiten und die zunehmende Armut erhält vor diesem Hintergrund eine noch tiefgreifendere Bedeutung, denn diese Menschen werden um ein Versprechen betrogen, das das mythische Amerika allen zu geben scheint. Konzepte wie *promise, dream, freedom, independence, equality* gelten in den USA offensichtlich nicht für alle Menschen gleichermaßen.
Die Vorstellung vom *American dream* ist nicht nur in vielen Lebensbereichen präsent – auch in Literatur und Kunst und im Bereich der *popular culture* findet immer wieder eine Auseinandersetzung mit diesem Konzept statt. Wenn Bruce Springsteen eine Platte mit dem Titel *Born in the USA* veröffentlicht, auf deren Hülle die amerikanische Flagge zu sehen ist, oder wenn ein Film mit dem Titel *Independence Day* in die Kinos kommt, dann wird hier bewusst (und erfolgreich) auf Ideen und Vorstellungen verwiesen, die konstitutiv sind für den *American dream.*
Ziel dieser Materialsammlung ist, Schülern und Schülerinnen die wichtigsten Aspekte, die in ihrer Gesamtheit das Konzept des *American dream* bilden, bewusst zu machen und damit Erklärungsmuster anzubieten, die zu einem vertieften Verständnis der amerikanischen Gesellschaft und Kultur führen können. Denn erst wenn eine Gesellschaft und Kultur sozusagen von innen heraus transparent geworden ist, kann wirkliche interkulturelle Kompetenz erworben werden.
Wichtig war aber auch, wie bereits im Titel des Heftes anklingt, nicht nur Material zum Idealkonzept des *American dream* zusammenzutragen, sondern auch eine kritische Auseinandersetzung damit zu ermöglichen. Wie sieht der Traum aus, was verspricht er, und wie steht es mit der Realität? Gilt der Traum für alle, immer noch?

Zum Einsatz dieses Heftes im Unterricht:
Bei der Zusammenstellung dieses Materials spielten mehrere Überlegungen eine wichtige Rolle:
Die ausgewählten Texte sollten neben den klassischen Texten zum Thema (wie z.B. die *Letters from an American Farmer* oder die Unabhängigkeitserklärung) viel neues, aktuelles Material bieten.
Wichtig schien auch, nicht zu lange Texte zusammenzustellen, die gut im Rahmen von einer oder zwei Unterrichtsstunden bewältigt werden können.
Ein weiterer Gesichtspunkt bei der Zusammenstellung war, eine große Vielzahl an unterschiedlichen Textsorten zu präsentieren. (Zeitungstexte, Sachtexte, Romanauszüge, Gedichte, Songtexte, Statistiken, Bildcollagen usw.), um möglichst viel Abwechslung in den Unterricht zu bringen.
Wo es sich anbot, wurde die Sammlung mit Bildmaterial angereichert, das methodisch sehr unterschiedlich genutzt wird. Oft dient es als Einstieg in eine Stunde und als Hinführung zum Thema. Andere Bilder und Zeichnungen wiederum sind eng auf das Textmaterial bezogen – als Ergänzung und Vertiefung oder als kritische Kontrastierung.
Alle Texte und Abbildungen sind mit Aufgabenstellungen versehen, die hoffentlich einen methodisch abwechslungsreichen Unterricht ermöglichen und viele Rede- und Diskussionsanlässe bieten. Bei diesen Aufgaben werden auch immer wieder sprachliche Aufgaben miteinbezogen, weil der Bereich Spracharbeit und Wortschatzarbeit im Unterricht aus Zeitgründen häufig etwas zu kurz kommt.
Meist sprechen die Aufgaben für sich und erfordern keine zusätzlichen Erläuterungen. Wo immer es sich jedoch anbot, wurden im Kommentar, neben kurzen Hinweisen und Erläuterungen zu den vorgelegten Texten und Materialien, auch Stichworte für mögliche Antworten aufgenommen.
Aufbau und Anlage des Heftes sollen dem Benutzer die größtmögliche Freiheit bei der Unterrichtsplanung lassen.
Die einzelnen Kapitel bilden in ihrer Gesamtheit eine Unterrichtseinheit, die die wichtigsten Aspekte des Themas *American dream* abdeckt.
Es lassen sich aber auch problemlos einzelne Materialien herauslösen, um damit schon vorhandenes Material oder Lehrbuchtexte zu ergänzen.
Wer die Lektüre einer Ganzschrift in den Mittelpunkt einer Unterrichtseinheit zum Thema *American dream* stellen will, findet ebenfalls Materialien zur Ergänzung und Vertiefung. So kann man etwa den Roman *The Tortilla Curtain* von T. C. Boyle, der hier im Heft anhand von zwei Textbeispielen vorgestellt wird, mit seinen Schülern lesen. Ergänzen ließe sich diese Lektüre dann durch Zusatztexte mit dem

Schwerpunkt „Einwanderung früher und heute". Aus der Fülle von vorhandenem Filmmaterial zum Thema *American dream* habe ich ein Video (vgl. A 19) ausgewählt, das sich sowohl für den Unterrichtseinsatz eignet als auch für den Lehrer (über die jeweiligen Bildstellen) leicht zugänglich ist. Zu diesem Video wurde ein Arbeitsblatt erstellt, das die Betrachtung des Videos begleiten soll und Diskussionspunkte für das anschließende Unterrichtsgespräch liefert.
Am Ende des Kommentars findet sich eine Liste von Filmen, die gut im Zusammenhang mit dem Thema *American dream* gezeigt werden können.

Sequence I: First approaches

Diese erste Sequenz enthält verschiedene, bewusst spielerisch gehaltene Vorschläge, wie man sich dem Thema *American dream* im Unterricht nähern kann. Es müssen durchaus nicht alle Arbeitsblätter dieser Sequenz eingesetzt werden, sondern der Lehrer kann sich, jeweils passend für seine Lerngruppe, aus diesem Angebot seinen persönlichen Einstieg zusammenstellen.

A 1 Your students and America

Dieses Arbeitsblatt eignet sich gut als Einstieg in das landeskundliche Großthema USA, weil der Lehrer durch die hier gesammelten Begriffe einen ersten Eindruck vom Wissen der Schüler über die Vereinigten Staaten bekommt. Einfache grammatische Strukturen (*What/Who is this?/Why do you consider this (person) typically American? – It's typical, because* ...) erleichtern die sprachliche Annäherung an das Thema.
Das Sammeln der Begriffe lässt sich sehr gut in Partner- oder Kleingruppenarbeit durchführen. Das Zusammentragen der von den Schülern gefundenen Begriffe findet dann im Plenum statt: entweder der Lehrer oder die Schüler tragen die Begriffe auf die Folie des Overhead-Projektors (OHP) ein. Der Lehrer kann Begriffe aus den *Suggestions* ergänzen, falls nicht alle Buchstaben von den Schülern abgedeckt wurden.
Im späteren Unterrichtsverlauf kann man noch einmal auf das *ABC of the USA* zurückgreifen. Wenn die Schüler eine genauere Vorstellung von dem Konzept des *American dream* haben, können sie die Begriffe herausfiltern, die im Zusammenhang damit stehen.

A 2 The American dream – some key expressions

Während das *ABC of the USA* noch alle Assoziationen zu Amerika abrief, beziehen sich die Begriffe in der Grafik konkret auf den amerikanischen Traum. Erstmals tauchen die Begriffe auf, die sozusagen das Gerüst des *American dream* bilden. Immer wieder werden die Schüler bei der Beschäftigung mit diesem Thema auf *Ellis Island, melting pot, independence* etc. stoßen. Deshalb ist es wichtig, sie gleich zu Anfang der Unterrichtseinheit einzuführen.
Das gemeinsame Erarbeiten lässt sich folgendermaßen gestalten: Der Lehrer legt die Grafik als Folie auf den OHP und fragt danach, welche Wörter den Schülern bekannt sind bzw. was sie mit ihnen verbinden. Bei Canaan kann der Lehrer durch gezielte Fragen helfen (*Has anyone heard of "Canaan?" Where? – It was the Promised Land in the Bible to which Moses led his people – What does Canaan symbolize? What is the connection to the US?*).
Die *Definitions* können danach an die Schüler ausgeteilt werden mit dem Arbeitsauftrag, die Texte kurz durchzugehen und sich einen Begriff auszuwählen, den sie anschließend der Klasse vorstellen und erläutern. Das geschieht am besten in Partnerarbeit.
Natürlich kann der Lehrer die beiden Blätter auch nicht verteilen und die Definitionen lediglich als Grundlage für seine Erklärungen verwenden.

A 3 Images of the American dream

Das Arbeitsblatt hat das Ziel, einige der Kernbegriffe des *American dream* (wie sie in A 2 erarbeitet wurden) weiter zu festigen. Die **erste Aufgabe** auf dem Arbeitsblatt, das Identifizieren der einzelnen Elemente, dürfte den Schülern nicht schwer fallen.

Elements of the Collage:
Page 10:
Fourth of July – Statue of Liberty – Buffalo Bill – Route 66 – Abraham Lincoln – Marilyn Monroe – Immigrants – Skyscraper – Dollar bill – Superman – Railroad – James Dean

Page 11:
Pioneers – American flag – Martin Luther King – John Wayne – Hollywood – Foreigners become Americans – American limousine – Astronaut on the moon – Capitol – American Indian – Mayflower

Aufgaben 1, 2 und 3 werden am besten in Partnerarbeit erarbeitet; Aufgaben 3 und 4 können erst in Kleingruppen und dann im Plenum bearbeitet werden. Da sich verschiedene Bilder gut unterschiedlichen Kategorien zuordnen lassen, entsteht hoffentlich ein reger Meinungsaustausch im Klassenzimmer.
Die Antworten auf die Fragen 5 und 6 werden – je nach Kenntnisstand der Schüler – unterschiedlich ausfallen.

Bei **Aufgabe 5** wären folgende Nennungen denkbar:
Equality: *Declaration of Independence, Civil Rights Movement*
Immigration: *Green card, Asian immigrants*
Liberty: *George Washington, Liberty bell*
Fortune: *Donald Trump, Bill Gates, Elvis Presley, Madonna, Wall Street, Broadway etc.*
Independence: *Boston Tea Party, Declaration of Independence*
Individualism: *Marlboro commercials*
Progress: *Silicon Valley, computers, hamburger*
Bei **Aufgabe 6** könnten u. a. genannt werden:
African Americans (slavery/discrimination) – Ku Klux Klan (xenophobia) – Indians (genocide) – guns, drugs, gangs (violence) Gulf War, Vietnam War – homelessness (inequality/poverty) etc.
Im Anschluss kann diskutiert werden, welche Rolle Bildsymbole innerhalb des Mythos vom amerikanischen Traum spielen. In Ergänzung dazu bietet sich auch der Vergleich/die Auseinandersetzung mit Deutschland (Aufgabe 7) an.

A 4 The American dream – what it's all about

Nachdem durch die vorangehenden Arbeitsblätter in die Thematik der Unterrichtseinheit eingeführt wurde, folgt mit dem Essay *Trying to Capture a Myth* ein Text, der als Überblick und Zusammenfassung des bisher Erarbeiteten gedacht ist.
Die Zitate, die dem Text vorangestellt sind, stammen aus dem bekannten Buch von Studs Terkel *American Dreams Lost and Found.* New York, Ballantine Books, 1981.
Der Text kann entweder im Unterricht behandelt oder als Hausaufgabe gestellt werden.

Mögliche Antworten auf die Fragen:
Aufgabe 2: *ll. 1–10: The concept has mythic qualities and is associated with many different aspects of American life.*
Aufgabe 3: *ll. 11–18: If a person works hard he/she can achieve his/her goals and improve his/her standard of living.*
Aufgabe 4: *ll. 30–44: On a political level, America was seen as an opportunity to correct the mistakes government and society had made in the "Old World." The poor Europeans emigrants also viewed America, the "New World," as the land of opportunity – a place where they could better their lives. Thus, the "New World" was constructed as a mythical counterpart to the "Old World."*
Aufgabe 5: *ll. 72–82: The American dream pervades many aspects of American life. Even though it is an idealized picture which does not portray the "real America," it sets the standard against which success and failure are measured.*
Aufgabe 6: *ll. 83–93: The Americans at home and the soldiers who fought in Vietnam believed they stood up for freedom and democracy. As the war continued the lines between "right" and "wrong" got blurred and many Americans argued that this war was about politics and power and not about defending democracy in Vietnam.*
Aufgabe 7: Hier sind viele unterschiedliche Antworten denkbar. (Vgl. die Antworten zu Aufgaben 5 und 6 in A 3).

Sequence II: Historical background

Wie schon in der Überschrift erkennbar, sollen in diesem Kapitel die historischen Wurzeln des *American dream* erarbeitet werden. Ein Großteil des Ideengutes, das sich im amerikanischen Traum manifestiert, hat seinen Ursprung in der Siedlungs- und Gründungsgeschichte der USA.

A 5 Columbus – or how it all started

Den Einstieg in die stärker historisch ausgerichteten Arbeitsblätter liefert ein Cartoon, der den Schülern kurz und auf spielerische Weise die Entdeckung Amerikas in Erinnerung rufen soll.
Wer möchte, kann mithilfe des Cartoons auch schon einen kritischen Blick auf die Entdeckung und Besiedlungsgeschichte Amerikas werfen. Der Karikaturist selbst lässt nämlich Columbus sagen: „Seht nur! Ein unberührtes Land … Wo ein jeglicher seiner Zukunft Herr, frei zu finden seines Lebens Glück. In einer Welt von Gerechtigkeit und Gleichheit für alle! … Schmeißt die Rothäute raus und los geht's!"

Es bleibt dem Lehrer überlassen, ob er diesen Text in den Unterricht einbezieht oder den Schwerpunkt ausschließlich auf die produktionsorientierte Aufgabenstellung legt.
Für die kritische Auseinandersetzung mit der Siedlungsgeschichte lässt sich auch gut der Cartoon auf A 14 heranziehen.

A 6 America – the New Israel

In diesem Text werden die religiösen Wurzeln des amerikanischen Traums thematisiert. Den frühen Siedlern, die ihr englisches Vaterland verließen, um Religionsfreiheit zu finden, erschien Amerika als *The Promised Land* oder *The New Canaan*. Sich selbst verglichen sie mit den Hebräern des Alten Testaments, die aus der ägyptischen Sklaverei auszogen, um in der Ferne das ihnen versprochene Gelobte Land zu finden. Dieses Selbstverständnis der frühen Siedler lebt bis heute weiter im amerikanischen Glauben, *God's chosen people* zu sein.
Der inhaltliche Schwerpunkt der Aufgaben liegt bei der Erarbeitung dieser religiösen Bezüge. Mithilfe der beiden Bibelzitate und der beiden Strophen aus einer in den USA äußerst populären Hymne sollen die Begriffe *God's chosen people* und *Promised Land* verdeutlicht werden.
Die Abbildung der *Pilgrim Fathers* kann als Einstieg in die Stunde dienen. Mit ihrer Hilfe kann an die englischen Koloniegründungen und an den berühmten *Mayflower Compact* erinnert werden. Sie zeigt die *Pilgrim Fathers* am 21. November 1620 an Bord der *Mayflower* vor der Landung auf Cap Cod, wie sie feierlich einen Bundesvertrag über die Errichtung eines puritanischen Gemeinwesens unterzeichnen.

Mögliche Antworten auf die Fragen könnten sein:
Aufgabe 1: *ll. 1–15: The pilgrims believed they were the people God had chosen in order to start a new civilization in America. The "New World" became their "Promised Land."*
Aufgabe 3: *ll. 27–31: George Washington led his people to independence like Joshua did with his. He was a key figure in the War of Independence, in which he fought some of the important battles. Then, he became the Unitied States' first President. Thus, he was a leader in a double sense.*
Aufgabe 4: *The vision of the New World as depicted in the hymn clearly shows religious undertones and very much resembles the notions of biblical paradise.*

A 7 The Declaration of Independence

Dieser Text gehört zu den Grundlagentexten, wenn es um die Geschichte der Vereinigten Staaten geht und darf deshalb hier nicht fehlen.
Die Kernbegriffe des *American dream* wie *equality, liberty, pursuit of happiness* sind in der Unabhängigkeitserklärung von 1789 formuliert, haben also ihren Ursprung im politischen Bereich. Die Schüler sollen diese Formulierungen kennen und ihre Wichtigkeit für das Konzept des amerikanischen Traums erklären können. Die Übersetzungsübung auf dem Arbeitsblatt dient dazu, den Schülern die zentralen Aussagen des Textes noch einmal bewusst zu machen. Die Aufgaben 5 und 6 können herangezogen werden, um die Aufmerksamkeit der Schüler auf die Diskrepanz zwischen den in der Unabhängigkeitserklärung postulierten Idealen und der Umsetzung dieser Ideale zu lenken. Die Ideale der politischen Väter der amerikanischen Nation hatten von Anfang an für bestimmte Gruppen keine Gültigkeit – von den Indianern ganz abgesehen.
Noch heute gelten für Menschen verschiedener Herkunft unterschiedliche Maßstäbe; und noch immer bestimmt der „WASP" (*White Anglo-Saxon Protestant Male*) die meisten Bereiche in Politik und Gesellschaft.

Mögliche Antworten auf die Fragen könnten sein:
Aufgabe 3: *Wir erachten folgende Wahrheiten als selbstverständlich: dass alle Menschen gleich geschaffen sind; dass sie von ihrem Schöpfer mit gewissen unveräußerlichen Rechten ausgestattet sind; dass dazu Leben, Freiheit und das Streben nach Glück gehören. Dass, um diese Rechte zu sichern, Regierungen unter den Menschen eingesetzt werden, die ihre rechtmäßige Macht aus der Zustimmung der Regierten herleiten. Dass, wann immer sich irgendeine Form der Regierung als diesen Zielen abträglich erweist, es Recht des Volkes ist, sie zu ändern oder abzuschaffen und eine neue Regierung einzusetzen.*
Aufgabe 4: *Equal station – nature's God – created equal – unalienable rights – life, liberty and the pursuit of happiness – free and independent states – the protection of divine Providence*
Aufgabe 6: *Pros: God created the white race to rule over the other races/the South needs their labor force, otherwise it will economically collapse/the slaves are well looked after by their owners (food/clothing etc.)/they are not capable to decide for or to take care of themselves/they will endanger and even destroy the white man's culture and lifestyle etc.*
Cons: Colored people are human beings with a soul like the white men/the slave system is outdated, the South

must seek economic change/no matter how well people are looked after they remain unfree as long as they aren't allowed to decide for themselves/this country is a modern and democratic one – its laws are based on equal rights for everyone etc.

A 8 What makes an American?

Wie begeistert die Kolonialisierung des amerikanischen Kontinents von den Europäern aufgenommen wurde, zeigt dieser Ausschnitt aus den Schriften eines Franzosen. Crèvecœurs euphorische Beschreibung der Möglichkeiten in der „Neuen Welt" sind entscheidend in die Vorstellungen des *American dream* eingegangen: Den Einwanderer erwarten Freiheit, Gleichheit und Prosperität – in einer Gesellschaft, die jeden nach seiner Fasson selig werden lässt. Und mit seiner Charakterisierung des „Amerikaners" formuliert der Franzose als erster das berühmte *melting-pot concept*, das lange Zeit das Selbstbild des Landes entscheidend bestimmte.
Crèvecœur beeinflusste nicht nur seine Zeitgenossen, seine Vorstellungen hallen noch im heutigen Amerika wider – vor allem in der politischen Rhetorik (vgl. A 15).
Aufgabe 4 soll den Schülern bewusst machen, dass in diesem Text das *melting-pot concept* beschrieben wird. Aufgabe 5 weist auf die inhaltliche Übereinstimmung zwischen Crèvecœurs Schilderungen und der in A 7 behandelten *Declaration of Independence* hin. Aufgabe 6 will zur kritischen Diskussion des Textinhalts anhalten.

Mögliche Antworten auf die Fragen:
Aufgabe 1: attachment … for: *connection, bond, ties to* – distinct: *special, different* – industry: *hard work, diligence* – frolicsome: *merry, happy, active* – entertain: *consider, to provide, to take on* – toils of a different nature: *struggle, work of another kind*
Aufgabe 3: *(ll. 3/4) …, the love of a few who are as poor as himself, … – (ll. 39/40) …; can it want something more attractive, interesting, seducing – (l. 43) … where crops grow which are lush, big, overflowing, wonderful – (l. 54) …, rewarded by life in which everything is provided for, rewarded by an abundant livelihood –*
Aufgabe 4: Relevante Textstellen: *(ll. 10/11) strange mixture of blood, which you will find in no other country – (ll. 16/17) leaving behind him all his ancient prejudices and manners – (ll. 22/23) here individuals of all nations are melted into a new race of men – (ll. 24/25) Americans are the western pilgrims – (ll. 30/31) here they are incorporated into one of the finest systems of population – (ll. 37/38) here the rewards of his industry follow with equal steps the progress of his labor – (l. 39) self-interest – (ll. 42/43) clear those fields whence exuberant crops are to arise – (l. 46) here religion demands but little of him – (ll. 49/50) the American is a new man, who acts upon new principles*
Aufgabe 5: *ll. 5/6: possession of land – ll. 15–18: progress (new society; democratic government), New World – ll. 22/23: melting pot (new race, new people) – ll. 25–28: pioneer spirit, westward expansion – ll. 37/38: progress, promise – ll. 38/39: individualism – ll. 40–44: pursuit of happiness – ll. 44–48: democracy, equality, liberty (no kings, no church nobility) – ll. 49/51: progress, manifest destiny*

A 9 America – land of hope

Mithilfe der Materialien dieses Arbeitsblattes kann der Text von Crèvecœur von A 8 weitergeführt und vertieft werden. Über Jahrhunderte weg war Amerika das gelobte Land, der Inbegriff des Versprechens eines freieren und besseren Lebens. Die *statue of liberty* war das Erste, was die Einwanderer sahen, die per Schiff nach Amerika kamen – die Verheißung für ein neues Leben. Und sie ist heute weltweit Symbol für Freiheit und Demokratie geblieben. So hatten, beispielsweise, die chinesischen Studenten bei ihrer Demonstration für mehr Demokratie auf dem Tiananmnen-Platz 1989 eine Nachbildung der Freiheitsstatue aufgestellt.
Anhand des Gedichtes und der Abbildung auf S. 22 lässt sich mit den Schülern rasch die Bedeutung der Einwanderung für die USA erarbeiten und darüber hinaus klar machen, welche Vorstellungen die Ankömmlinge aus der Alten Welt mit der Neuen verknüpften, nämlich Freiheit und Wohlstand.
Wer möchte, kann mithilfe des Cartoons schon kritisch hinterfragen, ob die Erwartungen der Einwanderer wohl immer erfüllt wurden. Die Karikatur wird nur dann verständlich, wenn ihr sprachlicher Bezug zum Gedicht von Emma Lazarus deutlich wird.
Die beiden Abbildungen auf S. 23 greifen noch einmal die Vorstellungen auf, die die Einwanderer hatten (und zum Teil noch haben). So zeigt die Zeichnung oben, wie sich die Menschen vor drohenden „Unwettern und Dämonen" ihrer Länder in die „Arche Amerika" retten, wo sie *Uncle Sam* mit offenen Armen empfängt. Auch hier schwingen wieder religiöse Untertöne mit: das gelobte Land erscheint als rettende Arche.
Das Foto einer Einwandererfamilie, das auf Ellis Island entstanden ist, und die dazugehörige produktionsorientierte Aufgabe eröffnet den Schülern einen affektiv-emotionalen Zugang zum Thema Einwanderung.

A 10 The concept of manifest destiny

Kaum ein anderes Element des amerikanischen Selbstverständnisses ist so schwer fassbar wie das des *manifest destiny.* Der Glaube, dass die Vereinigten Staaten anderen Ländern überlegen sind und die Aufgabe haben, den *American way of life* weltweit zu verbreiten, zieht sich durch die gesamte Geschichte des Landes. Der Gedanke, das auserwählte Volk zu sein (vgl. A 6), verstärkte die Vorstellung der *manifest destiny* noch.
War der Gedanke zunächst auf territoriale Ausdehnung der Landesgrenzen beschränkt (die Eroberung des Westens war mit ein Ergebnis dieser Vorstellung), so weitete er sich im Laufe der Jahrhunderte auf andere Bereiche aus und durchzog bald Kultur, Gesellschaft und Wissenschaft. Der Glaube an die eigene Überlegenheit und an die Verpflichtung, anderen Ländern „den richtigen Weg zu zeigen", ließen die USA bis heute immer wieder in das Weltgeschehen eingreifen. Sie handelten sich damit viel Kritik an dieser Rolle als „Weltpolizist" ein, und auch ihr so genannter „Kulturimperialismus" wurde ihnen vorgeworfen.
Der ausgewählte Sachtext mit den dazugehörigen Aufgaben soll Schülern helfen, das Konzept von *manifest destiny* zu erfassen, die historischen Auswirkungen zu erfassen und eine kritische Reflexion des Konzeptes in Gang zu bringen.
Mithilfe der Abbildung „Settlers trecking westwards" auf S. 25 wird die Aufmerksamkeit der Schüler auf die Besiedlung des Wilden Westens und die stete Ausdehnung der Grenze gen Westen gerichtet und so das Konzept des *manifest destiny* noch einmal an einem für die amerikanische Geschichte besonders wichtigen Beispiel veranschaulicht. Gleichzeitig bietet die Abbildung die Möglichkeit, zu erarbeiten, wie sehr der Zug nach Westen idealisiert und romantisiert wurde.

Mögliche Antworten auf die Fragen:
Aufgabe 1: *ll. 2–6: Historical events are being tangible; manifest destiny is the intangible ideology that underlies and shapes American history.*
Aufgabe 2: *Sullivan argued that the right to settle the entire continent was given to the Americans by God. According to Sullivan the Americans had the duty to expand superior rule over the entire American continent in order to bring liberty and democracy to other nations, as well.*
Aufgabe 3: Etappen der territorialen Ausweitung: *Texas, annexed as a state in 1845 – Utah, California, New Mexico, ceded by or purchased from Mexico 1848 and 1853 – Oregon territory relinquished by Britain in 1846 – Alaska and Hawaii, admitted as states in 1959. Other examples of US interference, which could be related to manifest destiny: Korea – Cuba crisis – Vietnam*
Aufgabe 4: *The concept of manifest destiny is a phenomenon which triggers the decisions and actions behind the historical dates. It is the driving force behind American history.*
Aufgabe 5: *All through the article the author assumes a rather neutral tone. He doesn't criticize the concept but just tries to describe it and its consequences. Only ll. 35/36 and ll. 43/44 may be understood as critical comments.*

A 11 Manifest destiny or imperialism?

Mit diesem Arbeitsblatt wird noch einmal versucht, anhand einer politischen Rede aus dem 19. Jahrhundert das Konzept des *manifest destiny* kritisch zu beleuchten.
In dieser Rede fordert der republikanische Senator Beveridge so deutlich wie kein anderer das Recht für die USA ein, territorial zu expandieren. Die Überheblichkeit und das Pathos in der Rede des Senators werden die Schüler vermutlich zu emotionalen Reaktionen provozieren, die dann durch die Fragen auf dem Arbeitsblatt in geordnete Bahnen gelenkt werden. Ziel ist, den Schülern klar zu machen, dass *manifest destiny* und Imperialismus eng beieinander liegen. Die Schüler sollen anschließend mithilfe der abgebildeten *Newsweek*-Titelseite die heutige Rolle der USA kritisch diskutieren.

Mögliche Antworten auf die Fragen:
Aufgabe 2: *Imperialism – policy of constantly extending a country's empire and/or its political, military, and economic influence.*
Aufgabe 4: *Beveridges's arguments: superior people (ll. 7–10) / imperial by their power and institutions (ll. 11/12) / heroic statesmen and armies (ll. 17–22) / visionary politicians and philosophers (ll. 23–26) / successful expansionism (ll. 37–49) / it is America's duty (ll. 74–78).*
References to God and religion pervade Beveridges's entire speech. It was God who had given the Americans the land and made them His chosen people. God's protection and benevolence gave the Americans the right to successfully pursue their imperialist policy. People such as Jefferson, Lincoln and Dewey were tools through which God executed His will. Thus, it would equal blasphemy if the American people did not continue their struggle for liberty and civilization.
Aufgabe 5: *Manifest destiny caused statesmen to support ideas of territorial expansion and soldiers to*

fight for the annexed land – great numbers of immigrants settled and cultivated the new land – politicians like Jefferson ignored the timid voices of the thirteen states' settlers and acquired new territory – the country needs to be cultivated and modernized – America must not only conquer the continent, but also demand its rights as a sea power – it is God's wish and doing that the US has become such a powerful imperial nation; it's the country's (manifest) destiny to become the world's driving force for democracy and liberty.

Sequence III: The dream today

Nach der historisch ausgerichteten Sequenz II geht es in diesem Kapitel um das Amerika der Gegenwart. Mit dem hier zusammengestellten Material sollen Facetten des amerikanischen Traums beleuchtet werden, wie sie das Leben des Einzelnen (A 12–14, A 19) und auch viele Bereiche der Gesellschaft prägen (A 15–18).

A 12 From rags to riches

Eine der häufigsten Antworten auf die Frage, was den amerikanische Traum ausmache, ist der Verweis auf materiellen Reichtum. Dabei geht es vor allem darum, dass jede(r) die Chance hat, erfolgreich zu sein. Der Mythos vom Tellerwäscher, der zum Millionär wird, ist für viele Amerikaner und Einwanderer grundlegende Lebensphilosophie: Wenn man es wirklich will, wenn man Risiken eingeht und sein Ziel immer vor Augen hat, dann kann man alles erreichen.
Der Glaube an diesen Mythos erklärt u.a. den Widerstand vieler Amerikaner gegen staatliche Absicherung, die sozialdarwinistischen Tendenzen und den radikalen Individualismus in den USA. Es gibt zwar nur wenige „lebende Beispiele", für die der Traum vom Reichtum wahr geworden ist, doch die wenigen reichen aus, um den Glauben an das „Land der unbegrenzten Möglichkeiten" zu festigen.
Zu Anfang der Stunde sollen drei Personen vorgestellt werden, die sich „hochgearbeitet" haben: Bill Gates als Gründer von Microsoft und einer der reichsten Männer der Welt, die schwarze Schauspielerin Whoopi Goldberg und die Gründerin einer der größten Kosmetikfirmen, Estee Lauder.
Mithilfe der biografischen Stichwörter können die Schüler mündlich einen kurzen Lebenslauf der drei Personen formulieren. Anschließend sollte herausgearbeitet werden, was alle drei Personen gemeinsam haben: dass sie nämlich Verkörperungen des amerikanischen Traums *From rags to riches* darstellen.
Als Projektarbeit eignet sich das Recherchieren nach anderen Amerikanern, die *from rags to riches* gelangten. Hier besticht vor allem das Internet als Informationsquelle. Sollten an der Schule keine Computer bzw. kein Internet zur Verfügung stehen, können die Schüler zu Hause recherchieren.

Hier ein paar Vorschläge:
Elvis, Madonna, Tina Turner, Louis Armstrong, Bruce Springsteen; Rap Stars wie *Ice-T, Coolio, Public Enemy; Michael "Air" Jordan, Michael "Magic" Johnson, Frank Capra, Steven Spielberg, Sylvester Stallone, Marilyn Monroe, Henry Ford, Louis B. Mayer (Metro-Goldwyn-Mayer), Oprah Winfrey (Talkshow), Walt Disney, Ray Kroc (Mc Donald's).*
Bei dem Versuch, Frauen oder „Nicht-Weiße" zu finden, fällt auf, dass der Traum vom Reichtum hauptsächlich für *White Anglo-Saxons* gilt (das Magazin *Fortune* weist in seiner Liste der Meistverdienenden nur 63 Frauen auf – und 2.257 Männer). Die Ausnahme bilden der Sport und die Musik: beide Bereiche bieten traditionell Aufstiegschancen für schwarze Amerikaner. Musik und Film – das „Entertainment" generell – ist auch eine Möglichkeit für Frauen, zu Ruhm und Reichtum zu gelangen. Ansonsten überwiegen die männlichen, weißen Kandidaten. Ein wesentliches Lernziel ist folglich die Erkenntnis, dass die Chancengleichheit eben nicht für alle gilt, sondern dass Rasse und Geschlecht die Aufstiegsmöglichkeiten einschränken.
Der Sachtext über *Social mobility in the US* stammt aus einer britischen Zeitung und beleuchtet die USA aus europäischer Sichtweise. Der Autor Jonathan Freedland untersucht die tatsächliche Dynamik des *American dream* innerhalb der Gesellschaftsordnung: Bewegen sich die Amerikaner wirklich von einer Gesellschaftsschicht zur anderen? Ermöglicht die vermeintlich klassenlose Gesellschaft jedem/jeder den Aufstieg?
Anhand dieses Textes soll erarbeitet werden, inwiefern sich Europa und die USA in ihrer Einstellung zu Reichtum, Erfolg und Herkunft unterscheiden. Da der Text relativ lang ist, wird zur Entlastung der Texterarbeitung eine *pre-reading activity* vorgeschlagen. Bevor die Schüler den Text ausgeteilt erhalten, bekommen sie den ersten Absatz als Lückentext vorgelegt und werden auf diese Weise erst einmal in die Behandlung des Textes eingestimmt.

Mögliche Antworten auf die Fragen:
Aufgabe 5: *the US seems to be free of class envy; no one resents a person for his/her success – it is not bad taste if*

people talk about money – Americans don't seem to be interested in equal distribution of wealth – in America, you will find very rich and very poor people – almost 40% of the Americans don't want government to close the gap between rich and poor – Americans accept inequality because they believe in the American dream – it seems strange to us, but the mythic quality of the American dream is still alive – even though it doesn't look like social mobility exists, statistics prove that poor people can better their status – the rags-to-riches myth works: four out of five millionaires started with nothing – money is at the center of America's social divisions – people with money do not necessarily show off their wealth in their appearance or behavior – one consequence is the lack of a welfare system – the underlying idea is the hope to get rich, not the protection of the poor.

A 13 An ordinary success story

Dieser Artikel aus einem Frauenmagazin nähert sich der Thematik *social mobility* über das Schicksal von Marinela Sue-Ho Reyes. Im Gegensatz zu den berühmten Repräsentanten des amerikanischen Traums wurde sie weder weltbekannt noch steinreich. Trotzdem hat sich auch für sie – in bescheidenerem Rahmen als etwa bei Bill Gates oder Whoopi Goldberg – ihr amerikanischer Traum erfüllt. Sie hat die Möglichkeit zu einer guten Ausbildung genutzt und auch ihre Kinder haben gute Aussichten auf eine bessere Zukunft und auf sozialen Aufstieg. Und damit wurde für sie ein zentrales Versprechen des *American dream* eingelöst – *progress* und *social mobility.*
Da der Text inhaltlich und sprachlich nicht schwierig ist, wird hier eine handlungsorientierte Vorgehensweise vorgeschlagen. Die Schüler erhalten den Artikel als Puzzletext und müssen in Partner- oder Gruppenarbeit die richtige Reihenfolge erarbeiten. Erfahrungsgemäß dürfte ihnen das keine großen Schwierigkeiten machen.
Darüber hinaus lassen sich mithilfe dieses Textes gut Informationen über das amerikanische Schul- und Bildungswesen erarbeiten.
Bei der Besprechung des Textes sollte auch darüber spekuliert werden, für welche Zielgruppe der Text wohl gedacht sein könnte. Ergebnis sollte sein, dass hier sicher für ein einfaches, wenig anspruchsvolles Publikum geschrieben wurde.

Mögliche Antworten auf die Fragen:
Aufgabe 1: elementary school: *the first school, from 6–9, 6–11, or 6–13, the system varies* – high school: *four- or six-year institution following elementary school* – boarding school: *(elementary or) high school where students receive lodgings* – junior college: *educational institution following high school, but only offering two-years' courses* – community college: *another name for "junior college"* – university: *institution which provides further education; either after high school or after college.*

A 14 Not all dreams come true

Nachdem bisher die Gewinner des *American dream* vorgestellt wurden, wenden wir uns nun mit dem Song von Bruce Springsteen den Verlierern zu. Anhand dieses Liedes können die Schüler erkennen, dass für viele Amerikaner der amerikanische Traum nicht in Erfüllung geht.
Lehrkräften, die eine größere Einheit zum *American dream* planen, kann ich den Kauf von Springsteens CD nur empfehlen, da sich fast alle Lieder für diese Thematik anbieten. Sämtliche Texte sind der CD beigefügt.

About the CD:
The Ghost of Tom Joad *was released in 1995 and is Springsteen's most recent album release (except a 4-CD box set of unreleased material in 1998). The title relates the CD to John Steinbeck's* Grapes of Wrath*: Tom Joad was the main character in this novel about one family's plight during the 1930s depression. Springsteen's move to California (another parallel to the Joads) has influenced not only the musical arrangements, but also some of the lyrics, which deal with "Southwestern problems" such as illegal immigration from Mexico. The protagonists of his songs are common people or even outsiders and criminals; people who are denied their share of the American dream.*

Eine *pre-reading activity* soll die Schüler auf das Thema des Liedes einstimmen. Anschließend wird den Schülern der Song vorgespielt, und sie sollen den Inhalt, so gut es geht, rekonstruieren. Der Lückentext wird ihnen erst beim zweiten Vorspielen des Liedes ausgeteilt. Die Aufgaben 5 bis 9 sollen den Textinhalt erarbeiten und zudem helfen, die literarische Anspielung auf John Steinbecks Roman *Grapes of Wrath* zu erkennen.

Mögliche Antworten auf die die Fragen:
Aufgabe 1: *rich – poor – no food – hunger – homelessness – Third World inequality – people begging – people sleeping in the street – money spent on weapons instead of food – child labor*

Aufgabe 5: *1. Walkin', goin' – verkürzte Formen / 2. chopper – Hubschrauber – helicopter / 3. kiddin' – jdm. etwas vormachen – to deceive s.o. / 4. nobody ... nobody – doppelte Verneinung – nobody – anybody / 5. drag – Zug (an der Zigarette) – draw / 6. 'round, 'neath – verkürzte Formen – around, beneath / 7. belly – stomach / 8. cop – policeman / 9. guy – man, person*
Aufgabe 6: *He wants to relate today's problems with poverty to other periods of hardship. He hopes to show that things haven't changed much since the 1930's. Many people have read the novel or seen the movie. They might associate certain senes/pictures with Springsteens's song.*
Aufgabe 8: *This bible verse refers to the Last Judgement. One angel is telling another angel to use his sickle to cut down the earth's grapes, which are ripe for harvest. The grapes symbolize the people who have forgotten God's word and are corrupted by the evil of the world. They are "ripe" because they didn't heed the call and repent their sins. The winepress of God's wrath will destroy them and cleanse the world in order to rebuild it.*
Aufgabe 9: *Tom Joad in the novel "The Grapes of Wrath" fights against "social sins" and the corruption of the heart. Springsteen uses the Tom Joad character in his song, because he views Tom's opponents as the same "grapes of wrath" that the angels want to destroy.*
Tom Joad symbolizes all the men and women who have fought for social justice in America.

Mithilfe der beiden folgenden Abbildungen kann noch einmal die kritische Auseinandersetzung mit dem „Land der unbegrenzten Möglichkeiten" im Mittelpunkt stehen. Beide Abbildungen zeigen Personen, für die der amerikanische Traum offensichtlich nicht gilt.
Bei der Behandlung des Bildmaterials steht die mündliche Arbeit im Vordergrund. Das Stilmittel der Ironie sollte anhand der oberen Abbildung erarbeitet werden. Die Aufgabe, einen Titel für das Foto zu finden, kann die Schüler dazu anregen, selbst Ironie „anzuwenden".
Der Cartoon ist gut geeignet, den Umgang der USA mit verschiedenen ethnischen Minderheiten zu problematisieren und kann noch einmal verdeutlichen, dass verschiedene Gruppen der Gesellschaft von Anfang an wenig Chancen hatten, ihren amerikanischen Traum zu leben.
Aufgabe 7 ermöglicht den Schülern einen affektiven Zugang zu den dargestellten gesellschaftlichen Randgruppen.

A 15 The challenge of the future

In den hier gewählten Auszügen aus der zweiten Antrittsrede des amerikanischen Präsidenten am *Martin Luther King Day* 1997 wird sichtbar, wie sehr sich die politische Rhetorik bei den Ideen des *American dream* bedient. Wenn es darum geht, möglichst viele Amerikaner anzusprechen, so verwenden Politiker oft Bilder, die dem nationalen Mythos entspringen. Begriffe wie *Promised Land, Founding Fathers, American dream* etc., verweisen auf ein gemeinsames Erbe, eine gemeinsame Geschichte und gemeinsame Wertvorstellungen. Diese Rückbezüge sind konstituierend für die USA, da sie aus sehr verschiedenen Kulturen erwachsen sind, die erst durch den Gründungsmythos zu einer Nation wurden.
Nachdem mit Frage 3 die Bilder und Begriffe markiert wurden, die sich auf den *American dream* beziehen, haben Fragen 4+5 das Ziel, die Unterschiede (und Gemeinsamkeiten) zwischen deutscher und amerikanischer Rhetorik zu erarbeiten. Wie reagieren die Schüler auf das Pathos der Rede? Empfinden sie Reden deutscher Politiker ähnlich? Welche Ziele verfolgt der Redner mit seinen Anspielungen auf Geschichte und Geschichtsmythos? Die Schüler sollen erkennen, dass die Arbeit mit sprachlichen Bildern wie den zuvor aufgelisteten ein typisches Merkmal für politische Rede ist, weil sie den Zuhörern ein breites Spektrum an Assoziationen und Interpretationen ermöglichen. Die Karikatur kann dazu benutzt werden, Clintons Rede kritisch zu beleuchten. Werden wirkliche Inhalte transportiert, oder erschöpft sich die Rede im Aneinanderreihen bloßer Floskeln?

Information on Clinton:
born 1946 in Hope/Arkansas – studied at Georgetown, Oxford (Rhodes scholarship) and Yale → law degree in 1973 – Arkansas Minister of Justice in 1976 – married Hillary Rodham in 1976; daughter Chelsea was born in 1980 – in 1978, Clinton became youngest governor, lost in 1980, but returned to office in 1982 – president of the National Governors' Association – announced his candidacy for President in 1991, won against his Democratic competitors – competed with Al Gore from Tennessee (vice presidency) against the Republicans George Bush and Dan Quayle → Clinton was elected President of the United States in November 1992 (youngest in history) – programs included (failed) attempt to reform the federal welfare and health insurance, allowing homosexuals into the military, and the American Free Trade Agreement

with Mexico and Canada (started in 1994) – leading role during the peace talks between the Palestinians and Israelis and the NATO operations in Bosnia – was re-elected in 1996 and started his second term with many new ministers – main goals during Clinton's second term were the national deficit, education, and the fight against violence, drugs and poverty – in 1998, Clinton was accused of sexual relationship with intern Monica Lewinsky – charged with perjury in January 1999, Clinton faced an impeachment trial before the Chief of Justice and the Senate – on Feb. 12, Clinton is acquitted of all charges.
(There was only one other impeachment trial in American history: in 1868, President Andrew Johnson was accused of aiding in Abraham Lincoln's assassination so he could move up to the top job. Johnson won by a single vote and was kept in office.)

Mögliche Antworten auf die Fragen:
Aufgabe 2:

line:	verb:	noun:
10	to extend	*extension*
12	to abolish	*abolition*
18	to choose	*choice*
20	*to solve*	solution
31	*to immigrate*	immigrant
33	*to pretend*	pretense
35	to destroy	*destruction*
57	to realize	*realization*
83	to know	*knowledge*
86	*to unite*	union

Aufgabe 3: *(l. 5) keep old democracy forever young – (l. 6) ancient vision – (l. 7) new promise – (ll. 9/10) we are all created equal – (ll. 11/12) our nation spread across the continent – (l. 20) We the American people – (l. 21) our founders – (l. 24) our common dreams – (ll. 27/28) one nation, one people, with one common destiny – (l. 31) new wave of immigrants – (l. 39) we shall overcome – (ll. 42/43) religious and political diversity – (l. 47) new vision of government – (l. 52) education – (l. 55) possibility – (l. 57) a nation ever moving forward – (l. 58) prosperity and power – (l. 60) progress – (ll. 71/72) Martin Luther King's dream was the American Dream – (l. 78) faith – (l. 84) our beloved country – (ll.87–89) America's bright flame of freedom spreading throughout all the world*
Aufgabe 6: *Clinton is portrayed as a blind man with dark glasses, searching his way to the speaker's desk in order to give his second Inaugural speech. Since his speech refers to the future – "a new promise" for the United States – the fact that he has no vision is used in a figurative sense.*

A 16 Winning is the only thing!

Nicht nur die Politik, sondern auch andere Lebensbereiche werden durch den *American dream* beeinflusst. Stellvertretend wird hier ein Auszug aus einem Sachbuch behandelt, der sich mit der Rolle des Sports in den USA auseinandersetzt. Anhand des gewählten Textausschnitt lässt sich verdeutlichen, wie wichtig in der amerikanischen Gesellschaft neben Freiheit und Individualismus das Streben nach dem Sieg. ist. Nur der Gewinner zählt.
Die Schüler sollen die amerikanische Einstellung zum Sport erarbeiten, mit der deutschen vergleichen und sich anschließend Gedanken machen, welche Rolle Sport in ihrem Leben spielt.

Mögliche Antworten auf die Fragen:
Aufgabe 3: regarded – *seen, viewed as* / outgrowth – *consequence, result* / devised – *thought up, invented* / ardent – *big, enthusiastic* / transpires – *becomes visible, happens* / constrained – *forced, compelled*
Aufgabe 4: *(See table.)*

Sport in the U.S.	**Sport in other countries** *(the opposite to the US is implied)*
– *failure is a person who settles for second best*	*participating and trying is more important than winning*
– *failure is a person who blames others for his or her shortcomings*	
– *winning is the only thing*	
– *value of individual achievement*	*focus on team*
– *intolerant of drawn games*	*many drawn games*
– *individual responsibility to make it on his/her own*	
– *qualities are determination, aggression, daring*	*not as aggressive*
– *highly legalistic approach*	
– *intolerance of ambiguity*	
– *for the masses, not for the knowledgeable few*	
– *family events and entertainment*	*either high society (tennis, golf) or male-dominated (soccer)*
– *instructing spectators about rules and players*	
– *contributes to the task of nation-building*	

A 17 The mythical West – a legend still alive

John Wayne symbolisiert einen wichtigen Aspekt des *American dream* – Pioniergeist bzw. *frontier spirit.* Nach der Eroberung des Westens wurde der Mythos im Western lebendig gehalten, und John Wayne war wohl der populärste aller Westernhelden – der Inbegriff des freiheitsliebenden Mannes, der sich für Recht und Gerechtigkeit einsetzt.
Der Textauszug lässt sich gut mit A 10 „The concept of manifest destiny" kombinieren.
Die Stunde setzt mit einer *pre-reading activity* ein. Die Aufgaben 5–7 sollen den Schülern Gelegenheit geben, eigene Kenntnisse und Vorstellungen einzubringen.

Mögliche Antworten auf die Fragen:

Aufgabe 2:
Auswahl möglicher Lösungen:

line:	word:	opposite:
4	to arrive	*to depart*
5	to reject	*to accept*
11	fixed	*loose*
18	urban	*rural*
18	freedom	*captivity*
20	to cease	*to begin*
39	to seize	*to let go*
45	to improve	*to get worse/ deteriorate*

Aufgabe 3: *(See table.)*

American - the West - the Frontier	European - the East - the City
displaced person – on the move – escapes enclosure – people of departure – lives with nature – leaves behind institutions (schools, libraries, government) – unspoiled and free to roam	*begins with a fixed place – settles down – searches community – lives in the city – creates institutions and sets rules for society – lives and works in closed-in places – corrupted by other humans and their way of living*

A 18 Space – the final frontier?

Nachdem der Westen erobert war, wurde der Weltraum zur neuen Herausforderung, zur neuen Grenze, die es immer weiter nach vorne zu schieben galt.
Jede Sendung der Serie „Raumschiff Enterprise" begann ursprünglich mit diesem Satz: *„Space – the final frontier …"* Die Abenteuer von Captain Kirk und all seinen Nachfolgern ähneln denen der Westernserien: Pioniere dringen in unbekanntes Land vor und finden dort fremde Völker. Das Weltall hat den Mythos vom Weste(r)n vielleicht nicht abgelöst, aber sicherlich ergänzt.
Die Fragen und Aufgaben zum Text sollen den Schülern deutlich machen, dass der *frontier spirit* im Weltraum weiterlebt und den Stolz und die Begeisterung der Amerikaner bei der ersten Mondlandung herausstellen.
Der Cartoon schlägt einen Bogen von der Entdeckung Amerikas bis hin zur Mondlandung und rundet damit diese Sequenz ab, die mit der Entdeckung Amerikas begonnen hatte.

Mögliche Antworten auf die Fragen:
Aufgabe 2: *Many people were waiting for the announcement. Regular business was interrupted. The Americans considered it a national achievement and were very proud and enthusiastic. It had been a national and scientific "mission." People everywhere were stunned.*

Aufgabe 3: *other frontiers: the geographical frontier moving westward – frontiers in science*
Aufgabe 5:
- *the last frontier – the cowboy changes into an astronaut*
- *progress and the faith in the future*
- *patriotism – the US as the Number One on the moon*
- *manifest destiny/expansionism – man's mission is not chained to our planet*
- *individualism – Armstrong, Aldrin and the others became heroes and idols*

Aufgabe 6 : *The 1960s in the US were restless times. The hippy and the student movements widened the gap between the generations, between politicians and the young Americans. The war in Vietnam escalated and its violence increased the anger the young people felt. The 1960s also were times of violence within the United States. Political leaders such as John F. Kennedy, Martin Luther King and Malcolm X were assassinated. The formerly peaceful student and civil rights movements grew more and more aggressive; radical groups like the "Black Panthers" and "The Weathermen" were founded.*
When US politics and society seemed to have failed, the successful Apollo mission brought a spark of hope and gave the Americans back some of their optimism and their belief in a better future.

A 19 Video: The American dream

Zum Abschluss der Sequenz kann ein Videofilm *The American dream* (Länge: 30 Minuten) eingesetzt werden, der sich noch einmal mit dem Alltag des durchschnittlichen Amerikaners beschäftigt. Drei Personen und ihre Einstellungen zum Leben in Amerika werden hier vorgestellt. Der Film lässt sich über die Landesbildstellen beziehen.
Um das Hörverständnis und die anschließende Diskussion zu erleichtern, sollten die Schüler zunächst die Fragen auf dem Arbeitsblatt durchlesen. So haben sie beim Anschauen des Videos klare Arbeitsaufträge, die sie anschließend zügig bearbeiten können. Ist die Zeit knapp, kann man die Beobachtungsaufträge von vornherein arbeitsteilig vergeben. Steht eine Doppelstunde zur Verfügung, kann man den Film zweimal vorspielen. Beim ersten Anschauen sammeln die Schüler zunächst einmal nur erste Eindrücke. Das Arbeitsblatt wird erst beim zweiten Sehen eingesetzt.

Antworten auf die Fragen:
a) Beach at Santa Monica, Beverly Hills
b) Radio announcer
c) Realtor – selling houses and apartments
d) Advertising
e) Inherited money (parents were rich) – expensive education – married
f) Marriage, parenthood ... not necessarily money
g) Move to the countryside and enjoy life

h) Actor/comedian
i) Cuba
k) Cubans and people with accent are stereotyped in films (gangsters)
l) 100%
m)Hard work, believe in yourself, believe you can make it
n) Ghettoblasters on the street

o) Student/lifeguard (to pay for college)
p) To become a teacher
q) Mother from Okinawa; father (Mexican marine) – met her mother on Okinawa, married and took her to the US
r) Japanese (discipline, motivation) and Mexican religion, honoring the elders)
s) Her friends feel the pressure (you have to be better than everyone else) – give up relationships and friends – LA is a big facade (looks are more important than character)
t) Because she came from a poor family ("It would be like going home.")

Sequence IV: Immigrants then and now

Seit Jahrhunderten kommen Menschen aus den verschiedensten Gründen in die Vereinigten Staaten mit der Hoffnung, dort ein besseres Leben zu verwirklichen. Diese Sequenz stellt Texte und Materialien bereit, die sich mit dem Thema Einwanderung beschäftigen. Der Schwerpunkt liegt dabei auf *immigration today*.

A 20 Old and new immigrants

Mithilfe der Abbildung lässt sich verdeutlichen, dass auch im Einwanderungsland USA Immigranten nicht immer gerne gesehen wurden. Die alt eingesessenen Bewohner (obwohl selbst als arme Schlucker ins Land gekommen, wie die Schatten hinter ihnen beweisen) wollen den erreichten Wohlstand nicht gefährden, indem sie ihn mit anderen teilen.
Die Tabelle informiert darüber, aus welchen Ländern die Einwanderer heute kommen. Wichtig ist, dass die Schüler auf die hohe Zahl mexikanischer Einwanderer aufmerksam werden. Damit wird die Lektüre der beiden Auszüge aus T. C. Boyles Roman *The Tortilla Curtain* sowie der Song *Sinaloa Cowboys* vorbereitet (vgl. A 24 und A 25), die die Probleme mexikanischer Einwanderer thematisieren.

A 21 Immigration from 1820–1990

Die Übersicht zur Einwanderung im letzten Jahrhundert verschafft den Schülern einen Überblick über Einwandererzahlen und -nationen. Sie kann auch als Grundlage für ein kurzes Einzelreferat dienen.

Billingsley versucht in seinem Artikel herauszuarbeiten, was das Besondere an den USA als Einwanderungsland ist. Er greift dabei auch auf die Idee des *melting pot* zurück: die Vorstellung, dass aus Menschen unterschiedlichster Herkunft – mithilfe des *American dream* – Amerikaner werden. Sein Text ist die moderne Entsprechung zu Crèvecœurs *Letters from an American Farmer* (vgl. A 8).
Eine ähnliche Idee wird im Cartoon umgesetzt – allerdings ein wenig kritischer, da die Einwanderer sich zu „Supermännern" wandeln.
Das Konzept des „Schmelztiegels" und seine kritische Hinterfragung können anhand dieses Materials sehr gut erarbeitet werden

Mögliche Antworten auf die Fragen:
Aufgabe 1: *The key element is freedom.*
Aufgabe 2: *It is the adoption of American principles that makes a person American. The desire for freedom and equality are central principles. Without fear of state or religious oppression people can prosper and live according to their talents – and, thus, become Americans.*

A 22 Immigrants and the American dream

Die Umfrage unter Einwanderern zeigt auf eindrucksvolle Weise, wie lebendig der amerikanische Traum noch heute für diejenigen ist, die in die USA auswandern. Wie schon in *One Mom's Pursuit of the American Dream* (vgl. A 13) wird deutlich, dass die Menschen, die neu in das Land kommen, eine klare Vorstellung davon haben, was der amerikanische Traum für sie bedeutet und warum sie in den Vereinigten Staaten leben wollen.

Mögliche Antworten auf die Fragen:
Aufgabe 1: 1. firm – *strong, unshaken* / 2. to blend – *to mingle, to mix together* / 3. estimate – *judging the size of something roughly* / 4. assessment – *evaluation, judgement, result* / 5. to focus – *to concentrate, to center* / 6. to favor – *to prefer, to like better* / 7. to decrease – *to become less* / 8. inherent – *natural, innate*
Aufgabe 2: *(See table.)*

questions	percentage
Do you want to stay in the US?/Do you like being an American?	*nearly 100%*
Would you like to raise your children in the US?	*54%*
Would you like to raise your children in your homeland?	*33%*
Do you prefer the US when it comes to job opportunities?	*over 80%*
Do you agree that if someone works hard he/she can better him-/herself?	*93%*
Do you believe your children will have a better life in the US than you?	*70%*
Is the level of political freedom better in the US than in your homeland?	*75%*
Did you feel welcome when you first came to the US?	*80%*
Do you feel welcome today?	*90%*
Do you favor assimilation of different cultures in the US?	*59%*
Do you think the expression "melting pot" is an accurate description of the US today?	*75%*
Should legal immigration remain at its present level – or even be increased?	*59%*

Aufgabe 4: *Leaving behind your native country and emigrating to a foreign land is a very decisive step. People might not like to admit that they've taken the wrong decision.*

A 23 Immigration since 1970

Dieser kurze Zeitungsartikel aus der *Los Angeles Times* verdeutlicht eine gewisse Besorgnis über die Einwanderungstendenzen der letzten dreißig Jahre. Die Zahlen zeigen, dass sich die amerikanische Gesellschaft bereits verändert hat und sich längerfristig noch stärker verändern wird. Die lange Vorherrschaft der *White Anglo-Saxons* wird durch die wachsenden Zahlen anderer ethnischer Gruppen gefährdet. Im Südwesten der USA sind das in erster Linie Einwanderer aus spanischsprachigen Ländern.

Mögliche Antworten auf die Fragen:
Aufgabe 1: 1. is going through = *present progressive: something that is going on "around now"* / 2. has transformed = *present perfect: process which has started in the past, continuing up to the present* / 3. attained by = *passive as reduced relative clause ("which has been attained by")* 4. are included = *passive simple present: the figures are part of the survey right now* / 5. did react = *simple past: action happening in the past*
Aufgabe 4: *The author tries to assume a neutral tone but some phrases and expressions (l. 6: dramatically affirm; l. 27: enormous increases; l. 37: tide of immigrants; l. 42–44: immigrant pool – poorer, less educated) reveal that he isn't quite unbiased.*

A 24 Illegal immigration

Viele der Einwanderer kommen illegal in die USA; vor allem die schwer zu überwachende Grenze zu Mexiko wird genutzt, um in die Vereinigten Staaten zu gelangen.
Die Menschen, die mit dem Traum vom großen Reichtum in die USA kommen und erkennen müssen, dass es ein Traum bleiben wird, stehen im Mittelpunkt des Songs *Sinaloa Cowboys* von Bruce Springsteen. Seine „Cowboys" sind zwei junge Mexikaner, die illegal über die Grenze nach

Kalifornien kommen, um dort ihr Glück zu machen. Sie verdienen zwar viel Geld in einem illegalen Labor, in dem offensichtlich Drogen produziert werden. Aber beide riskieren ihre Gesundheit, und Louis bezahlt mit seinem Leben, als die illegale Drogenküche explodiert.
Zuerst sollte das Lied ohne Text vorgespielt werden mit dem Auftrag an die Schüler, einzelne Wörter oder Sätze, die sie heraushören, zu notieren. Es folgt das Zusammentragen der „Fundstücke" und erste Mutmaßungen über Inhalt und Thema des Liedes. Beim zweiten Hören haben die Schüler den Lückentext vor sich und versuchen, möglichst viele der Lücken zu füllen. Es folgen einige Fragen zum Textverständnis: *Why do Miguel and Louis decide to go to the US? – What kind of work did they do when they reached California? – What kind of job do "the men from Sinaloa" offer them and why do they take it? – What happens to Louis?*
Ergänzend ist bei den Fragen und Aufgaben eine kurze Meldung über einen Gesetzesentwurf hinzugefügt, der das Ziel verfolgte, die illegale Einwanderung in Kalifornien (vor allem aus Mexiko) einzuschränken. Dieser Text soll verdeutlichen, wie nah Springsteens Geschichte der Wirklichkeit kommt.

Mögliche Antworten:
Aufgabe 11: 1. ineligible – *not qualified* / 2. to back – *to support* / 3. to approve – *to ratify, to confirm* / 4. to reject – *to turn down, to refuse* / 5. in the wake of – *close behind, immediately after*

A 25 Haves and have-nots

Wir bleiben in Kalifornien und bei der illegalen Einwanderung.
In dem 1996 erschienenen Roman *The Tortilla Curtain* schildert T. C. Boyle das Schicksal von Candído, einem illegalen mexikanischen Einwanderer, der mit seiner blutjungen schwangeren Frau América am Fuß eines Cañons haust. Nachdem Delaney Mossbacher, ein junger Kalifornier, Candído angefahren und verletzt hat, kreuzen sich beider Wege immer wieder. Es mehren sich die Übergriffe auf die Luxussiedlung, in der Delaney mit seiner Frau Kyra wohnt. Die Mossbachers sehen ihre geschützte Welt zunehmend bedroht von den fremden Gestalten, die verzweifelt um einen kleinen Teil des amerikanischen Traums kämpfen.
Der erste Auszug schildert Américas erste Begegnung mit dem Leben, das sie sich in den USA erträumt hat.
Der zweite Ausschnitt beschreibt das Leben der Familie Mossbacher, die alle Privilegien des Wohlstandes genießt.
Durch die Gegenüberstellung der beiden Welten – bzw. der beiden Ausschnitte – erkennen die Schüler, wie groß der Unterschied zwischen Arm und Reich in den USA ist und wie gering die Chancen der Armen sind, ihren amerikanischen Traum zu verwirklichen.
Die Abbildung auf Seite 59 kann als Einstieg in die Textarbeit genutzt werden.

Mögliche Antworten auf die Fragen:
Text I
Aufgabe 1: 1.gazing out on – *looking* / 2. trails that plunged through the brush – *dug* / 3. the color was striking – *impressive, amazing* / 4. His eyes darted everywhere – *shot, moved quickly* / 5. the leafy dolorous hell of the canyon – *painful*
Aufgabe 2: *(See table.)*

time and place	about América	about Candído
- *San Fernando Valley* - *night/early morning* - *they left their camp in the canyon and are walking next to the street/highway* - *hills, nature, coyotes*	- *pregnant* - *exhausted* - *fears that immigration control will catch them* - *fears that a car will hit them*	- *in a hurry* - *urges América to move on* - *knows the way*
- *they enter the residential area: pretty houses, pretty street* - *in the past, they lived in Tepoztlán, Cuernavaca, Tijuana – places which were as horrible as the Canyon*	- *exhilarated, excited* - *curious* - *admiring the beautiful houses* - *is fascinated, like paradise* - *yearning for comfort*	- *worried sick and silent* - *anxiously checking the area* - *introduces her to downtown* - *trying to pull her away*

Aufgabe 5: *Just like the "Iron Curtain" used to separate Eastern and Western Europe the "Tortilla Curtain", as the North American–Mexican border is called, separates Mexico from the USA.*
Aufgabe 6: darkness clung to the hills – *personification (=a thing is given human attributes)* / rustled in the brush – *onomatopoeia (words which imitate sounds)* / San Fernando Valley opened up like an enormous glittering fan – *simile (=comparison with "as/like")* / Sherman Way ... Sherman Way – *anaphora (repetition of expressions)* / adorable, linda, simpática, cute – *aggregation of words with similar meaning* / hell ... paradise – *contrast (=opposing ideas)*

Text II
Aufgabe 4: *A computer has a keyboard. Since Delaney mentions that his wife is the person who earns the money, it cannot be a highly-paid job (computer business). Actually, Delaney writes articles for nature magazines.*
Aufgabe 6: *The author doesn' t show open contempt for his figures in the excerpt. But you can easily infer from some textpassages that he doesn't like his characters very much. For example Kyra's exaggerated concern for wholesome food, her plastic containers with vitamin pills and her way of not taking her son seriously prevent the reader from sympathizing with her. When an author presents unlikeable characters readers won't be much inclined to read about these people.*

Sequence V: Nightmare Vietnam

Kein Ereignis hat den Glauben vieler Amerikaner an ihr Land so erschüttert wie der Krieg in Vietnam vor 35 Jahren. Konnte die Regierung anfangs die Bevölkerung noch davon überzeugen, dass es um die Befreiung eines Landes und den Kampf gegen den Kommunismus ging, so wurde schon nach wenigen Jahren deutlich, dass die Mehrheit in In- und Ausland diesem Krieg immer skeptischer gegenüberstand.
Als erster *televised war* erschütterte Vietnam das amerikanische Volk mit Bildern und Informationen, sodass Mitte der Sechzigerjahre der Rückzug aus Vietnam gefordert wurde. So verwischt die Grenzen zwischen Freund und Feind in Vietnam selbst waren, so umstritten war auch Amerikas Rolle als „Retter der Demokratie". Gut und böse, richtig und falsch waren nicht mehr auseinander zu halten – vor allem nicht für die, die in Vietnam kämpften. Und sicherlich waren die Soldaten in Vietnam diejenigen, die am meisten verloren.
Diese Sequenz soll zeigen, wie das Selbstverständnis und -bewusstsein der Amerikaner in den Sechziger- und Siebzigerjahren ins Wanken geriet. Nach dem Boom der Vierziger- und Fünfzigerjahre zerstörte der Krieg auch Grundlagen des amerikanischen Traumes wie z. B. den Nationalstolz und die Überzeugung, die USA seien das Ideal einer auf Gerechtigkeit und Demokratie beruhenden Gesellschaft. Die Attentate auf John F. Kennedy, Robert Kennedy und Martin Luther King, das Massaker amerikanischer Soldaten an vietnamesischen Zivilisten in My Lai sowie der Tod amerikanischer Studenten, die bei einer Antikriegs-Demonstration an der Kent State University von der Nationalgarde erschossen wurden, stürzten die Vereinigten Staaten in eine Phase der Selbstzweifel, die erst in den Achtzigerjahren durch Ronald Reagan mit seiner Politik der Stärke und seinen Forderungen nach mehr Nationalbewusstsein und -stolz beendet wurde.

A 26 The war in Vietnam – historical background

Die Landkarte und der Überblick über die geschichtlichen Zusammenhänge und Ereignisse bilden den Einstieg in diese Sequenz.
Die Informationen können entweder als Grundlage für einen Lehrervortrag bzw. ein Einzelreferat genutzt oder an alle Schüler ausgeteilt werden. Zu einzelnen Ereignissen können ebenfalls Referate verteilt werden.
Da im Internet relativ viel Material zum Vietnamkrieg zu finden ist, sollten die Schüler aufgefordert werden, selbst Informationen über den Krieg im Internet zu recherchieren.

A 27 Vietnam poetry

Die beiden Gedichte sind authentische Texte von Vietnamveteranen. Beide Gedichte beziehen sich nicht auf Ereignisse im Krieg, sondern auf die Zeit nach der Rückkehr aus Vietnam. Im ersten werden die Erlebnisse des Krieges zu konkreten Albträumen, die sich auch nach langer Zeit nicht abschütteln lassen. Auch im zweiten Gedicht, das aus der Sicht einer Frau geschrieben ist, gelingt es dem Kriegsheimkehrer nicht, in das alltägliche Leben zurückzufinden. Wie viele andere versucht auch der Betroffene in diesem Gedicht vergeblich, die

traumatischen Erinnerungen an seine Zeit im Dschungel zu verarbeiten. Die Unfähigkeit, das Gesehene zu vergessen, trieb viele der Heimkehrer an psychische Grenzen. Oft half auch die Flucht in Drogen oder professionelle Betreuung nicht, sodass nicht selten als letzter Ausweg der Selbstmord die einzige Lösung schien. (Der Historiker Walter Capps schreibt in seinem Buch *The Unfinished War – Vietnam and the American Conscience*: "(...) that since 1975 there have been as many suicides among Vietnam veterans as there were combat fatalities during the war itself." (S. 1))
Die Aufgabenstellungen, die die beiden Gedichte begleiten, zielen nicht auf eine detaillierte literarische Interpretation der beiden Texte. Die Schüler sollen vielmehr mithilfe der Aufgaben ein Stück weit begreifen und nachfühlen können, welch gravierenden Folgewirkungen der Krieg auf das Leben der Teilnehmer hatte.
Die beiden Fotos des *Vietnam Memorial* helfen verdeutlichen, wie präsent dieser Krieg in der Erinnerung vieler Amerikaner noch ist.

Mögliche Antworten auf die Fragen:
Aufgabe 3: Mögliche Adjektive:
depressing – sad – gloomy – melancholic – tense – person feels lost/haunted/alone/helpless
2nd stanza: *more peaceful – calm – yearning*
Aufgabe 5: Mögliche Assoziationen: *night – sleep – American dream world – nightmare – pyjama – dreams come true – quiet – sweat – ghost – waking up – screaming – the unconscious – rest – peace – colors – ...*
Aufgabe 6: *prom= a big, festive dance for the senior students who leave high school. The students dress up in expensive clothes; sometimes they rent limousines to pick up their dates in. Usually, one girl and one boy are voted "prom king and queen".*
fit = *outburst of emotion; maybe "white" and "black" refer to fits of anger and depression, respectively*

A 28 Dreams destroyed

Um Erinnerung und Verarbeitung geht es auch in der Autobiografie des Vietnam-Veteranen Ron Kovic, der – wie viele seiner Altersgenossen – vom Heldentum träumt und begeistert in den Krieg zieht (1. Ausschnitt), um dann körperlich und seelisch verkrüppelt in ein Amerika zurückzukehren, das seine „Helden" ignoriert oder sogar ablehnt (2. Ausschnitt). Der Gegensatz zwischen dem Amerika seiner Kindheit und dem, was er als Kriegsveteran kennen lernt, lässt Kovic fast zerbrechen. Im letzten Moment schafft er den Sprung aus Isolation, Depression und Selbstmordgedanken und wird einer der politisch aktivsten Vietnamveteranen, die gegen den Krieg und die Behandlung der Überlebenden durch die Regierung protestieren.
Der Roman besticht in erster Linie durch seine Authentizität und Unmittelbarkeit. Kovics Schilderungen sind die eines wütenden, einfachen Mannes, der mit zwanzig im Krieg seine Beine verloren hat und von seinem Land aufs Bitterste enttäuscht wird. Das Buch heißt übrigens *Fourth of July*, weil Kovic am Unabhängigkeitstag geboren wurde.
Obwohl das Buch stellenweise die Leser sowohl inhaltlich als auch sprachlich schockiert, halte ich es für eine geeignete Lektüre, falls man sich länger mit dem Thema Vietnam beschäftigt. Auch die Verfilmung von Oliver Stone mit Tom Cruise in der Titelrolle bietet viele Arbeits- und Diskussionsanlässe für den Englischunterricht.
Die beiden Textauszüge wurden so gewählt, dass sie den Kontrast zwischen dem Idealismus des *All American boy* und der Desillusionierung des Veteranen zeigen. Die Textauszüge werden in arbeitsteiliger Gruppenarbeit behandelt. Jede Gruppe erhält einen Textauszug und soll entweder in Einzel- oder in Partnerarbeit die Arbeitsaufträge bearbeiten. Anschließend informieren sich die Gruppen gegenseitig über die Textauszüge und können darüber spekulieren, was wohl alles vorgefallen ist, um den Erzähler zu diesem totalen Meinungs- und Stimmungsumschwung zu bringen.

Mögliche Antworten auf die Fragen:
Text I:
Aufgabe 3: magnificent: *excellent – fine – perfect – glorious – fantastic – dazzling – splendid – terrific – marvellous – superb*

Text II:
Aufgabe 3: awesome: *very frightening – terrorizing – scaring – stunning – horrifying – shocking – appalling*

A 29 Surviving Vietnam

Bruce Springsteens Lied *Born in the USA* ist auch noch heute vielen Jugendlichen bekannt. Aber – wie auch beim Erscheinen 1984 – wird das Lied von fast allen missverstanden und gilt als patriotisches Bekenntnis.
Dass es das nicht ist, wird erst bei genauerer Beschäftigung sichtbar; zu dominant sind Musik und Refrain, sodass der Text nur selten wahrgenommen wird.
Besonders empfehlenswert ist die Arbeit mit dem

dazugehörigen Video (nähere Angaben S. 95), das bei vielen Bildstellen ausgeliehen werden kann. Das Video verstärkt zunächst durch Springsteens Auftreten den patriotischen Eindruck. Aber es erzählt dann auch andere Geschichten, indem es zahlreiche Bilder in den Konzertmitschnitt integriert. Anfangs sind es positive Bilder aus Kindheit und Jugend; später tauchen zunehmend negative Bilder (Arbeitslosigkeit, Soldaten, Vietnam, Friedhof) auf, sodass sich aus diesen Bildfetzen eine ganze Lebensgeschichte zusammensetzen lässt.

Den Schülern wird zuerst das Lied vorgespielt. Ihre ersten Eindrücke sollen sie in einer kleinen Skizze festhalten. Anschließend wird das Video gezeigt, und die Schüler sollen zusammentragen, welche Bilder im Video erscheinen und anschließend ihre Bilder mit denen des Videos vergleichen (Aufgaben 3–5). Erst dann wird den Schülern der Liedtext ausgeteilt mit dem Auftrag, den Inhalt kurz zusammenzufassen. Normalerweise sind die Schüler bei der genauen Textlektüre sehr überrascht, wie kritisch der Songtext ist.

Mögliche Antworten auf die Fragen:
Aufgabe 2: *1. flag 2. factory 3. small town houses 4. boy's birthday 5. old photo 6. young man 7. prom night 8. fairground (carousel) 9. street (rearview mirror) 10. car 11. car for sale 12. welfare line 13. man at shooting gallery 14. soldiers 15. veterans (military tattoo) 16. Asian (Vietnamese) child 17. Arlington Cemetery 18. factory 19. girl on bycicle 20. worker 21. man with beer 22. girl 23. baseball players 24. woman in doorway 25. Springsteen and flag*
The images tell a second story about what it's like to live in the USA: youth and innocence (ll. 1–7) are destroyed by war and unemployment (ll. 8–18) – even though life goes on (ll. 19–23), the scepticism remains (ll. 24/25).
Aufgabe 4: *The flag appears in the beginning: there it sets the scene, because it tells the viewer where everything is taking place. It symbolizes the USA and everything associated with that nation.*
At the end, Springsteen is shown in front of the flag. When he turns his head, he looks sceptical. This time the flag symbolizes the dark sides of American history.
Aufgabe 9: *merry – jovial – buoyant – exhilarated – radiant*
Aufgabe 10: A little angry: *upset – annoyed – displeased – grudging* / rather angry: *angry – irritated – aggravated – incensed – irascible* / extremely angry: *furious – enraged – infuriated – berserk – rancorous – livid – frenzied*

Sequence VI: Is the dream still alive?

Diese Sequenz enthält verschiedene Vorschläge, wie sich eine Unterrichtseinheit zum Thema *American dream* abschließen lässt.

A 30 Is a new dream necessary?

Obwohl MacLeish diesen Essay bereits vor fast 60 Jahren verfasst hat, gelang es ihm, ein zeitloses Plädoyer zu formulieren. In dem hier abgedruckten Ausschnitt fasst MacLeish die Essenz des *American dream* zusammen, verurteilt den nostalgischen Blick zurück und fordert, die Ideale des Traumes der heutigen Wirklichkeit anzupassen.
Mithilfe des Textes können die Schüler noch einmal die wesentlichen Ideale des amerikanischen Traumes zusammenfassen, aber auch über mögliche neue Interpretationen in der Zukunft nachdenken. Da sich dieser Text auch für sprachliche Analysen eignet, beziehen sich die ersten Fragen des Arbeitsblattes auf den Stil des Autors. Nach der inhaltlichen Erarbeitung folgen dann die übergreifenden Fragen, die auf die gesamte Unterrichtsreihe ausgeweitet werden können.

Mögliche Antworten auf die Fragen:
Aufgabe 3 (Auswahl): a) accumulation: ll. 37–41: *the industrial nation of huge machines, the limitless earth …*; l. 70: *a great builder, a maker, a shaper*
b) anaphora: ll. 7–11: *because …*; ll. 12–21: *Because …*; ll. 22–24: *The courage of … the courage of …*
c) amplification: l. 2: *… imagination. Men imagined …*; ll. 6/7: *… imagination of the minds – because they imagined;* ll. 12/13: *And what was true of the continent was true of the Republic.*
d) contrast: ll. 49: *Is the fault within the machines or with ourselves?* ll. 81–85:
e) rhetorical question: ll. 42–45 *Is it inconceivable …?*; ll. 45–48: *Is it certain..?*

A 31 Test your knowledge

Das Kreuzworträtsel ist in erster Linie als Auflockerung des Unterrichts gedacht. Es dient zwar auch der Wiederholung einzelner Aspekte und Begriffe, die mit dem *American dream* zu tun haben; aber es sollten hier Spaß und Neugier im Vordergrund stehen.

A 31

	A	B	C	D	E	F	G	H	I	J	K	L	M	N	O
1	P	O	T			A	A		A				V	A	
2	R			L	I	N	C	O	L	N		E	T		I
3	O		M		N					Y		L		A	M
4	G		I	N	D	I	V	I	D	U	A	L	I	S	M
5	R	A	T		E		I					I			I
6	E				P	I	L	G	R	I	M	S		E	G
7	S		H		E		E	R		N			P		R
8	S	T	A	I	N			A	B	S		E	M	M	A
9			V		D		T	V		C	A			I	N
10	C	R	E	V	E	C	O	E	U	R		W	E	S	T
11	O		N		N		I			I		A		S	
12	L	T			C	O	L	U	M	B	U	S		I	T
13	L	O	C	K	E			S	E	E		P		O	
14	E		A				F	U	N	D		S	O	N	S
15	G		P		O	N		R					U		T
16	E		I		H	A	P	P	I	N	E	S	S		A
17	S	A	T			T			C	O	L		T	A	R
18		F	O	U	R	T	H		O		V			L	
19	A	L	L		N	Y		I	N	D	I	A	N	S	
20	R			G	A		U	S			S			O	R

A 32

A 32 Is the dream still alive?

Die Zeichnung, die die Freiheitsstatue als internationale Vermittlerin des amerikanischen Demokratiegedankens darstellt, thematisiert noch einmal das Selbstverständnis der USA wie auch ihre Beziehungen zu anderen Ländern. Was in Sequenz II als *manifest destiny* einer kritischen Betrachtung unterzogen wurde, erscheint hier in positivem Licht. Die Schüler sollten anhand der Zeichnung noch einmal rekapitulieren, welche Werte Amerika vertritt und ob die USA überzeugend sind in ihrer Vorreiterrolle als freiheitlich-demokratische Weltmacht.
Mit diesen Überlegungen lässt sich eine Reihe zum amerikanischen Traum sinnvoll abschließen. Die Schüler sollten nun in der Lage sein, differenziert Stellung zu nehmen und eine persönliche Beurteilung zu formulieren. Mithilfe des kurzen Textes von Jonathan Freedland kann die Aussageabsicht des Cartoons kritisch relativiert werden.

Damit der Abschluss der Unterrichtseinheit nicht zu trocken ausfällt, wird mit Aufgabe 5 eine kreative Übung vorgeschlagen, die den Schülern sicher viel Spaß macht und die sich gut in Partnerarbeit durchführen lässt.

Mögliche Antworten zu den Aufgaben:
Aufgabe 3: *The Statue of Liberty symbolizes freedom and democracy, which are central to the American constitution and the American self-image. The "flame of freedom" and with it the spirit of democracy is passed to other nations which are on their way to democracy.*
Aufgabe 5: Die Schüler können entweder selbst etwas zeichnen oder geeignetes Material aus Zeitschriften ausschneiden. Die Möglichkeiten, diese Zeichnung zu ironisieren, sind unbegrenzt. *Hamburger, Mickey Mouse, Coke, guns, cowboy hats – politicians – immigrants and so on.*

Filme zur Thematik:

Die hier aufgelisteten Filme sind meist über die Landesbildstellen, größere Videoläden oder Bibliotheken mit englischsprachigen Videos zu beziehen. Ich habe versucht, mich auf eine kleine Auswahl zu beschränken; sicherlich gibt es weitaus mehr geeignete Filme.

1. dokumentarisch

Domesticating a Wilderness (1974)
zur Besiedlung des Westens

Huddling Masses (1974)
zur Einwanderung im 19. und frühen 20. Jhdt.

Martin Luther King – The Legacy of a Dream (1983)
schildert die Bürgerrechtsbewegung der Schwarzen von 1955–1978

A Family Farm in Kentucky (1991)
thematisiert amerikanische Sichtweisen zum Thema Familie, Glück und Erfolg in Verbindung mit dem Leben auf dem Land

The Mejias from El Salvador to Los Angeles (1991)
sehr gutes Portrait einer Einwandererfamilie und ihrer Sicht der USA als Wunschheimat

America the Way I See It (1995)
wendet sich gegen (europäische) Vorurteile gegenüber dem „American way of life" und versucht eine objektive Darstellung der USA seit dem 2. Weltkrieg

2. allgemein

Mr. Smith goes to Washington (1939)

The Grapes of Wrath (1940)

The Great Gatsby (1974)

Death of a Salesman (1985)

Uncle Tom's Cabin (1987)

Field of Dreams (1989)
schöner Beitrag zum Thema „Sport and the American dream" – nicht nur für Baseballfans

Far and Away (1992)
ein irisches Paar, das im 19. Jhdt. sein Glück in der Auswanderung nach Amerika sucht

Malcom X (1992)

American History X (1998)

American Beauty (2000)

3. Western

Red River (1948)

High Noon (1952)

Fast alle Filme von John Ford (*Stagecoach, Rio Grande, The Searchers, The Quiet Man* etc.) zelebrieren Land und Individuum und eignen sich zur Analyse des Genre.

Dances with Wolves (1990)

4. Vietnam

Coming Home (1978)

Rambo I (1984)

Platoon (1986)

Gardens of Stone (1987)

Born on the Fourth of July (1989)

Das Video „The American Dream" ist entweder über das Medienzentrum Rheinland/Landes- und Stadtbildstelle in Düsseldorf oder über die FWU in München (Bestellnummer 4200988) erhältlich.
Das Video zum Bruce Springsteen-Song findet sich auf dem Video anthology 1978-88 und ist über Amazon.de erhätlich.

Internet-Adressen zum Thema:

Viele der Beiträge in diesem Heft wurden mithilfe des Internet recherchiert. Aus diesem Grund habe ich hier die wichtigsten und ergiebigsten Adressen zusammengefasst. Obwohl einige der Seiten im Laufe der Zeit entweder verlegt oder entfernt werden, halte ich diese Liste trotzdem für sinnvoll und hilfreich: sowohl Schüler als auch Lehrer sollten das Internet als Informationsquelle nutzen.

www.historychannel.com

arbeitet mit Suchbegriffen – alle möglichen Themen – Ausschnitte aus berühmten Reden – Materialien konkret für den Unterricht

http://wilstar.com/holidays/july4.htm

4th of July-Page mit historischen Dokumenten (*Mayflower, Independence, Washington* etc.), Texten und Musikbeispielen historischer Lieder

http://wilstar.com/holidays/index.html

Infos über alle anderen amerikanischen Feiertage (mit netten Quizfragen und Spielen)

http://www.colonialhall.com/biography.asp

Kurzbiographien zu allen Unterzeichnern der Unabhängigkeitserklärung und der Verfassung

http://www.ushistory.org/documents/declaration.htm

Website der *Independence Hall Association* in Philadelphia – u.a. Infos zum Unabhängigkeitskrieg und zu Benjamin Franklin

http://americanhistory.about.com

amerikanische Geschichte – Links zu anderen guten Homepages

http://xroads.virginia.edu/~HYPER/hypertex.html

Kurzbiographien verschiedener amerikanischer-Schriftsteller – Hypertexte zu und Auszüge aus einigen Werken

http://www.filmsite.org/grap.html

Website zum Film von Steinbecks Roman